# HARD GOALS

---

## THE SECRET TO GETTING FROM WHERE YOU ARE TO WHERE YOU WANT TO BE

---

## MARK MURPHY

New York   Chicago   San Francisco   Lisbon   London   Madrid   Mexico City
Milan   New Delhi   San Juan   Seoul   Singapore   Sydney   Toronto

**The McGraw·Hill** Companies

1 2 3 4 5 6 7 8 9 10 11 12 13 14 15   QFR/QFR   1 9 8 7 6 5 4 3 2 1 0

ISBN   978-0-07-175346-3
MHID        0-07-175346-X

This publication is designed to provide accurate and authoritative information in regard to the subject matter covered. It is sold with the understanding that neither the author nor the publisher is engaged in rendering legal, accounting, securities trading, or other professional services. If legal advice or other expert assistance is required, the services of a competent professional person should be sought.

> —*From a Declaration of Principles Jointly Adopted by a Committee of the American Bar Association and a Committee of Publishers and Associations*

**Library of Congress Cataloging-in-Publication Data**

Murphy, Mark A.
     Hard goals : the secret to getting from where you are to where you want to be / by Mark Murphy.
          p.    cm.
     Includes bibliographical references.
     ISBN 978-0-07-175346-3 (alk. paper)
     1. Goal (Psychology)    2. Motivation (Psychology)    3. Employee motivation.    4. Achievement motivation.    5. Goal setting in personnel management.    I. Title.

BF505.G6M87    2011
153.8—dc22                                                          2010029794

To Andrea, Isabella, and Andrew

# Contents

# Acknowledgments

I hate to be cliché, but there really are too many people to thank individually for making contributions to this book. My team of several dozen researchers and trainers, and each of our hundreds of fantastic clients, deserve a special thank-you. This book, and the research behind it, wouldn't exist without all of their efforts.

I would also like to highlight a few individuals who made special contributions to this particular book.

Andrea Burgio-Murphy, Ph.D., is a world-class clinical psychologist, my wife and partner through life, and my creative sounding board. Since we started dating in high school I have learned something from her every single day. My personal and professional evolution owes everything to her.

Lyn Adler is an exceptional writer who has worked with me for years. Lyn's assistance made it possible to distill mountains of research and interviews into this contribution to the science of goals.

Nicole Jordan, one of my vice presidents, took on special assignments filling in for me while I was immersed in the writing of this book. The assignments were HARD, and her performance was outstanding.

Corey Laderberg, Sarah Kersting, Kelly Love, and Jim Young are all members of the Leadership IQ team who deserve a special thank-you for their extra effort to help make this book possible.

Dennis Hoffman is an extraordinary CEO and entrepreneur whose friendship and counsel have significantly improved all of my books, including *HARD goals*. John Sheehan is a great friend and the smartest data mind I know; his insights always improve the quality of my research. And Elaine L'Esperance, Anthony Nievera, Phil Rubin, Sue Hrib, Dave Brautigan, Kevin Andrews, Ned Fitch, and Tom Silvestrini are all accomplished executives who have helped shape my thoughts on HARD Goals.

Mary Glenn, senior editor at McGraw-Hill, deserves a very special thank-you for recognizing the need for this book and making the process fast and smooth. After working with Mary and the team at McGraw-Hill, it's very clear to me why the best thinkers sign with them.

## FOR MORE INFORMATION

You can find free downloadable resources including quizzes and discussion guides at the HARD Goals website: hardgoals.com.

# Introduction

## HARD Goals—The Science of Achieving Big Things

I know something about you: you want to do something really significant with your life. Whether you want to double the size of your company, lose 20 pounds, run a marathon, advance your career, or transform the whole darn planet, you want to do something big and meaningful with your life. You want to control your own destiny and know that your life has a deep purpose.

I know this about you because you're reading this book. Some people are scared by this book; they don't want big goals or big achievements. They just want to pass the years, and they don't much care if they never taste even a little greatness. But that's not you, and you are the reason I wrote this book.

With all the challenges and opportunities facing our companies, families, careers, personal lives, and even our countries, we could use some really big achievements. But where do these big achievements come from? Why is it that some people achieve so much, while others are left spinning their wheels? Well, we can look to real achievers, in every walk of life, for the answer.

There's the woman at work who lost (and kept off) 20 pounds *and* got promoted to upper management *and* who finds time to attend all the big events at her kids' school *and* is gearing up to run her fourth marathon this year. There's the guy down the street who amassed $2 million in the bank—on a schoolteacher's salary. Then there's the entrepreneur who started a business during one of the worst recessions ever and grew sales by 1,200 percent in the first year. And, of course, there are famous CEOs like Steve Jobs and Jeff Bezos, the kind of folks who blow our minds with their amazing and innovative products again, and again, and again.

Are these superachievers just more motivated? Or are they more disciplined? The answer to both questions is yes, but not in the ways you might think. What these people have—what anyone who's ever tasted greatness has—is HARD Goals.

---

## THERE'S A GOAL FOR THAT

What are HARD Goals? The short answer is that HARD Goals are goals that are Heartfelt, Animated, Required, and Difficult (thus the acronym HARD). But that's not really an answer, so let me explain.

Your goals are one of the few things you truly control in this world; you can set them to achieve virtually anything you can imagine. To paraphrase Apple's famous line: If you want to lose weight: there's a goal for that. If you want to double your company's revenue: there's a goal for that. If you want to improve your personal finances: there's a goal for that. If you want to reform the world's financial system, avoid oil spills, shrink deficits, and accelerate the world's economies: there are goals for all those things too.

But much like the iPhone made us rethink the phone, so too will HARD Goals make us rethink goals. These aren't your typical goals. In fact, extraordinary goals are so different from the average person's goals that it's almost criminal to use the word *goal* to describe them both. The kinds of goals that lead to iPads, marathons, financial freedom, and weight loss stimulate the brain in profoundly different ways than the goals most people set. In nearly all cases where greatness is achieved, it's the goal that drives motivation and discipline—not the other way around.

---

## IT'S MORE THAN JUST HAVING GOALS

Almost everyone has set a goal or two in his or her life. Every year more than 50 percent of people make New Year's resolutions to lose weight, quit smoking, work out, save money, and so on. A majority of employees working for large companies participate in some kind of annual corporate and individual goal-setting process. Virtually every corporate executive on earth has formal goals, scorecards, visions, and the like. And who among us hasn't fantasized about having more money, a better body, more success at work, a swankier house, and so forth? All of these are goals.

And yet, notwithstanding the ubiquity of goals, many of us never achieve our goals. And the goals we do achieve often fall far short of extraordinary.

My company, Leadership IQ, recently studied 4,182 workers from virtually every industry to learn about their goals at work. What we discovered might not shock you, but it will probably dismay and disturb you: only 15 percent of people believed that their goals for this year were going to help them achieve great things. And only 13 percent thought their goals would help them maximize their full potential.

How can this be? There's copious self-help literature that tells us if we write down our goals, our dreams will come true. Corporations have formal goal-setting systems, like SMART Goals, to help employees develop and track their goals. And we've practically institutionalized New Year's resolutions. There's no shortage of goals in this world. So why aren't we all "blowing the doors off" every day? The short answer is that most of our goals aren't worth the paper they're printed on (or the pixels that display them).

## WHAT DO STEVE JOBS AND A THREE-YEAR-OLD HAVE IN COMMON?

Let me show you the inadequacy of our goals via a weird question: What do Steve Jobs and a three-year-old have in common? I know, it's a bizarre question and at first glance it doesn't seem like they have anything in common. But dig a little deeper, and it turns out that their goals are pretty similar. Oh sure, Steve Jobs wants to reinvent entire industries with his iPad and iPhone and iWhatever-comes-next, and that three-year-old probably just wants the cookie sitting on the counter. But mentally, they're using very similar systems, and tapping (and extending) the full potential of their brains.

First, their goals are *Heartfelt*. Steve Jobs and the toddler both have deep emotional attachments to their goals. What they want will scratch an existential itch. Steve has said the iPad is the most important work he's ever done, which is exactly how that three-year-old feels about nabbing the cookie. Both the iPad and the cookie represent a level of purpose and meaning that is impossible to shake off or walk away from.

Second, their goals are *Animated*. There are lively and robust images dancing through both their minds. Steve Jobs didn't write a number on a little worksheet and say, "657,000 iPads sold, that's my goal." He saw a movie in his head that showed people perusing newspapers, reading books, watching movies, and more, all with his marvelous tablet. He saw what the device looked like and how people would use it, right down to the emotional reaction people would have when they first took it out of the box—just as that three-year-old sees a far-away glimpse of a marvelous round disc that sparkles in the light the way only the crystalline structure known as sugar can. He can't describe exactly how it's going to taste (his vocabulary hasn't yet caught up to his palette), but he can imagine how great he's going to feel with that circle of sweetness in his mouth. Until his goal is attained and that cookie is his, the three-year-old's whole universe revolves around this picture in his mind.

Third, their goals are *Required*. They simply *must* achieve these goals, or their respective worlds will end—their survival depends on achieving these goals. It's rumored that Steve Jobs was working on the iPad while recovering from a liver transplant. And anyone with kids knows that toddlers who don't get their way truly believe the world is ending.

And finally, their goals are *Difficult*. There are no small, achievable, easy goals for these two. Nope, they want to enter uncharted territory, whether that's transforming how we get information or venturing to a spot in the kitchen that's twice as high as any place they've been before (remember, a toddler falling off the kitchen counter is like you falling off the roof of your house). Both situations are a bit scary, and these two will have to learn all sorts of new skills to make their goals a reality, but they're both alive and buzzing with the challenge.

Whether intentionally or intuitively, Steve and the toddler have harnessed the four essential components of extraordinary goals: they're Heartfelt, Animated, Required, and Difficult. And thus we call them HARD Goals. When you're emotionally connected to your goal, when you can see and feel your goal, when your goal seems necessary to your survival, and when your goal tests your limits, your brain will be alive—neurons literally lighting up with excitement.

This is the characteristic that distinguishes high achievers from everyone else. It's not daily habits, or raw intellect, or how many numbers you can write on a worksheet that decides goal success; it's the engagement of your brain. When your brain is humming with a HARD Goal, everything else you need to take your goal and run with it falls into place. But when your brain is ho-hum about your goals, all the daily rituals and discipline in the world won't help you succeed.

So why don't the rest of us achieve our goals like Steve Jobs and that kid who wants the cookie? The answer is because most people set woefully inadequate and incomplete goals. And sadly, this is often by design. For example, many businesses use a goal-setting process called SMART Goals. They set goals that are Specific, Measurable, Achievable, Realistic, and Time-Limited. For starters, goals that are Achievable and Realistic are diametrically opposed to Difficult goals—a critical element for engaging your brain. Steve Jobs has made a career out of doing things others said couldn't be done, and trust me, no goal he's ever set is going to pass the Achievable and Realistic test for a SMART Goal.

And even a factor like Specific, which sounds OK, can suck the life out of a goal. For most people, Specific means turn your goal into a number and jot it down (for example, I want to lose a specific weight, like 27 pounds). But that definition of "specific" pales in comparison to the intensely pictured animated goals of achievers like Jobs and others. Sure they've got a number, but they know what their body will look like 27 pounds from now, what clothes they'll be wearing, even how they'll feel when they no longer carry the weight. For them, 27 pounds isn't an abstract concept or a number on a form; it's a vision into the future that feels so real, it's as if it's already happened.

Some people and organizations get so hung up on making sure their goal-setting forms are filled out correctly that they neglect to answer the single most important question: Is this goal worth it? And then, if it is "worth it"—if it's a goal worthy of the challenges and opportunities we face—we need to ask, How do we sear this goal into our minds, make it so critical to our very existence that no matter what obstacles we encounter, we will not falter in our pursuit of this goal?

## YOU'VE DONE IT BEFORE (AND IT WAS GREAT)

Notwithstanding the inadequacy of many goals, I do have some good news: everyone has the capacity to set the kind of goals that generate greatness. How do I know? Because you've done it before.

Think about the most significant goal you've ever achieved. Maybe you ran a marathon, doubled your company's revenue, lost 30 pounds, or invented the coolest product in your industry. Now ask yourself these questions:

- Did this goal challenge me and push me out of my comfort zone?
- Did I have a deep emotional attachment to the goal?
- Did I have to learn new skills to accomplish it?
- Was my personal investment in this goal such that it felt absolutely necessary?
- Could I vividly picture what it would be like to hit my goal?

I'd be willing to bet that the goal that drove your greatest achievement was an incredibly challenging, deeply emotional, highly visual, and utterly necessary goal. I'll bet your mind was alive and buzzing with the thrill of it. And I'll also put my money on how, after you hit your goal, you were as fulfilled as you've ever been.

One of the most important findings from our research on goals is that people who set HARD Goals feel up to 75 percent more fulfilled than people with weaker goals. While we might silently hope that these super-high achievers are really unhappy inside ("Oh sure, she's got everything, but I'll bet she's really miserable"), the truth is these folks are actually a lot happier than their underachieving peers.

---

## WHAT THE WORLD NEEDS NOW IS HARD, HARD GOALS

With a nod to Burt Bacharach and Hal David, I'd suggest that the one thing there's just too little of right now is HARD Goals. As I write this book, there is no shortage of enormous challenges facing us individually and collectively. We're dealing with big issues like terrorism, wars, economic collapse, oil spills, corruption, deficits, unemployment, health care problems, and to top it off, the bulk of people in the world are either starving or becoming obese. And while we're trying to tackle these collective challenges, some of us individually are looking for jobs, contemplating running a marathon, trying to quit smoking, going back to school, getting healthy, trying to advance our careers or grow our businesses, and more.

So the question becomes, how do we meet big challenges? Do we tackle big challenges with even bigger thinking, courage, ambition, and resolve—also known as HARD Goals? Or do we pretend the challenges we face aren't really all that big? Maybe we deny they exist, or we just blame others, or we make excuses why we can't tackle them, or we just freak out and go hide in the corner. Or maybe we hope against hope that if we create a little mini-goal that's nice and easy, we can get through it all with a few baby steps.

The one thing that has kept modern civilization going as long as it has is that every so often we get a leader that knows how to set HARD Goals. The HARD Goal in Abraham Lincoln's Gettysburg Address steeled our resolve to fight so that "government of the people, by the people, for the people, shall not perish from the earth." John F. Kennedy's HARD Goal asked the nation to "commit itself to achieving the goal, before this decade is out, of landing a man on the moon and returning him safely to the earth." Ronald Reagan's HARD Goal demanded, "Mr. Gorbachev, tear down this wall!" Winston Churchill's HARD Goal made clear that "whatever the cost may be, we shall fight on the beaches, we shall fight on the landing grounds, we shall fight in the fields and in the streets, we shall fight in the hills; we shall never surrender."

Listen, I know it's a truly unsettling world right now. But you and I both know that denial, blame, excuses, and anxiety are not going to make it any better. We need to harness the energy of this moment, scary though it may be, and turn it into greatness. Whether we're going to grow our company, lose weight, run a marathon, or change the whole darn world, we're going to have to saddle up a HARD Goal and ride that sucker at a full gallop.

---

## GETTING STARTED

So where do we go from here? How do you recapture the incredible feeling of those past glories and create that same greatness and happiness in the here and now? In short, how do you set and achieve HARD Goals?

Here's how the chapters break down.

## Chapter 1: Heartfelt

If you don't care about your goals, what's going to motivate you to try and achieve them? In Chapter 1, you'll learn how to use the latest psychological science to develop deep-seated and heartfelt attachments to your goals on levels that are intrinsic, personal, and extrinsic. And you'll learn to use these connections to naturally increase the motivational power you put behind making your goals happen. You'll be able to go from a nagging sense of, "I really need to see this goal through (but I really don't feel like mustering up the energy to make it happen)" to, "I want what this goal promises more than anything, and nothing is going to get in my way of making it happen."

## Chapter 2: Animated

In Chapter 2 you'll learn how to create goals that are so vividly alive in your mind that not to reach them would leave you wanting. Using visualization and imagery techniques employed by some of the greatest minds in history (like Albert Einstein, inventor Nikola Tesla, physicist Richard Feynman, and more), we'll look at a host of ways to sear your goal firmly into your brain including perspective, size, color, shape, distinct parts, setting, background, lighting, emotions, and movement. It's the stuff of geniuses, and now it's yours to use as well.

## Chapter 3: Required

Chapter 3 is geared toward giving procrastination (which kills far too many goals) the boot. Using cutting-edge techniques from new sciences like behavioral economics, you'll learn how to convince yourself and others of the absolute necessity of your goals. You'll also discover ways to make the future payoffs of your goals appear far more satisfying than what you can get today. This will make your HARD Goals look a whole lot more attractive and amp up your urgency to get going on them right now.

### Chapter 4: Difficult

A big question facing any HARD Goal setter is, how hard is hard enough? You don't want things to be so difficult that you give up, any more than you want to feel so unchallenged that you stop trying. In Chapter 4, you'll learn the science of constructing goals that are optimally challenging to tap into your own personal sweet spot of difficulty. You've done great things in your life already, so we'll access those past experiences and use them to position you for extraordinary performance. Whether you're an undersetter or oversetter, after you read Chapter 4, you'll know exactly where your goal-setting comfort zone is and how to push past it (and face any fears that pop up along the way) in order to attain the stellar results you want.

---

## IF YOUR GOAL IS GOOD ENOUGH . . .

Let me leave you with one last thought: In certain business circles, it's become accepted wisdom that execution is somehow more important than vision. There are clichés aplenty about how it's better to fully implement a half-formed strategy than it is to half-implement a fully formed strategy. To put it in the language of this book, we might say that some people believe that implementing the goal is more important than creating the goal. And while it's true that execution and implementation are important, this idea misses one absolutely critical reality: if your goal is powerful enough, implementation won't be such a big problem.

If my goal was to eat more chocolate cake, I wouldn't need to worry too much about my cake-eating execution plan because I'd be so motivated to achieve the goal that there's no way I'd mess up its implementation. If my goal was to enjoy more amorous encounters with my wife during the week, you'd better believe I wouldn't fail to execute. If the goal is meaningful enough, you will execute.

This is true even for a goal that's less fun, but similarly emotionally powerful—like writing this book. This book is being written on a deadline amidst a period of explosive growth for my company (some of which is attributable to my previous book, *Hundred Percenters*). I am pushing myself to my very limits to finish this and everything else I've got going on (heck, it's 2 A.M. as I write this sentence). But my execution isn't waning for a second because I believe in this book heart and soul (heartfelt). I can vividly picture everything from people reading the book to the impact it's having on their lives (animated). It's as necessary to my existence as breathing (required). And it is forcing me, and all the people who work for me, to grow in ways I never would have imagined (difficult).

People spend way too much time trying to figure out how to trick themselves into implementing mediocre goals. What we need instead is extraordinary goals—HARD Goals. Listen, all the daily rituals in the world won't help us achieve greatness if the very goal we're trying to habitualize is weak. Do we really think that Steve Jobs, or Jeff Bezos, or Google's founders resort to little gimmicks to accomplish their goals? (Seriously, do we have the iPad, Kindle, and Google search engine because somebody put a sticky note on a fridge?) Or do we think that they're so deeply connected to what they're doing, that their goals are so important and meaningful to them, that they'll swim through a pit of alligators to fulfill those goals?

As soon as you opened this book, I knew you were after greatness, significance, and meaning and that you've got the talent and mind-set to achieve it. Now, what I'm going to give you in this book is the ways to make your goals worthy of your natural gifts. Because when your talent meets a HARD Goal, greatness is sure to follow.

Let's get started.

## QUIZ

Everybody loves quizzes, so let's start with one. The following 12 statements are designed to help you assess the quality of your goals. (If you want a more in-depth quiz, check out the website at www.hardgoals.com.)

To begin, think about a particular goal you'd like to achieve (you can take this quiz every time you need to assess a goal).

For each statement, give yourself a score from 1 (which means never) to 7 (which means always). For example, if I were to respond to "When I flip a coin, I correctly guess heads or tails," I would give myself a score of 4 because I correctly guess "heads or tails" about half the time (and 4 is the halfway point between 1 and 7).

If I were to consider "I love eating cauliflower," I would score this item 1 because, well, I really don't like cauliflower (and 1 means never).

And finally, go with your first response; don't second-guess your answers.

1. Something inside of me keeps pushing me to achieve this goal, even when things get in my way.
2. When I think about this goal, I feel really strong emotions.
3. I mentally own this goal; it doesn't belong to my boss, spouse, doctor, or anybody other than me. Even if somebody else initially gave me the idea for it, it's 100 percent my goal now; I own it heart and soul.
4. My goal is so vividly pictured in my mind that I can tell you exactly what I will be seeing, hearing, and feeling at the precise moment my goal is attained.
5. I use lots of visuals to describe my goal (such as pictures, photos, drawings, or mental images).
6. My goal is so vividly described in written form that I could literally show it to other people and they would know exactly what I'm trying to achieve.

7. I feel such an intense sense of urgency to attain my goal that postponing or pausing even one day is not an option.

8. Even if the full benefits of achieving my goal are a ways off, I'm still getting benefits right now, while my pursuit of this goal is still in process.

9. The payoff from attaining this goal far outweighs any costs I have to incur right now.

10. I'm going to have to learn new skills before I'll be able to accomplish this goal.

11. My goal is pushing me outside my comfort zone; I'm not frozen with terror, but I'm definitely on "pins and needles" and wide awake for this goal.

12. When I think about the biggest and most significant accomplishments throughout my life, this current goal is as difficult as those were.

## Scoring

Here's how to score your quiz.

Total your score for items 1 through 3 (your score could be as low as 3 or as high as 21). This is your Heartfelt score.

Total your score for items 4 through 6 (your score could be as low as 3 or as high as 21). This is your Animated score.

Total your score for items 7 through 9 (your score could be as low as 3 or as high as 21). This is your Required score.

Total your score for items 10 through 12 (your score could be as low as 3 or as high as 21). This is your Difficult score.

Once you've got your scores, you're ready to plot them. Use the Scoring Grid on page 19 and plot each of your four scores (Heartfelt, Animated, Required, and Difficult). See the Sample Grid on page 18 as a guide.

Most people are more naturally inclined toward certain aspects of goal setting. For example, some do really well at creating a heartfelt connection to their goals but fall short on making them difficult. Others have goals that are absolutely required but not particularly well animated. We all have strengths and weaknesses when it comes to setting goals, and that's what this quiz highlights. Just note that for a goal to have the best chance of success, every dimension has to be in the HARD Goal Zone.

In an ideal world, every aspect of your goals will fall into the HARD Goal Zone. This means you have a score of 20 or 21 for each dimension. When all of your scores are here, you're in great shape. Now you just need to tweak and refine your goals, keep a close eye on them, and start implementing.

Some scores may fall in the Zone of Concern. This means your scores fall in the range of 13 to 19. While your goals are within striking distance, any aspect of your goal that falls in this zone needs some work before it's ready for prime time.

And finally, you may see some scores in the Red Alert Zone, which means your scores are 12 or below. Any aspect of your goals that falls in this zone needs rethinking. Even one dimension with scores here can derail an otherwise solid goal. So before you begin to implement this goal, take some time to focus on anything in the Red Alert Zone. It's a "Red Alert" because even if you had three aspects in the HARD Goal Zone, any score in the Red Alert Zone would weigh down your entire goal like an anchor.

## Sample HARD Goal Scoring Grid

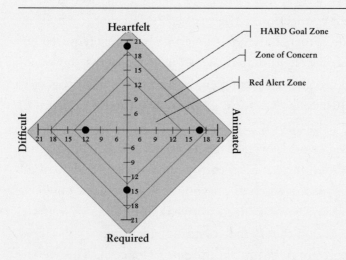

## HARD Goal Scoring Grid

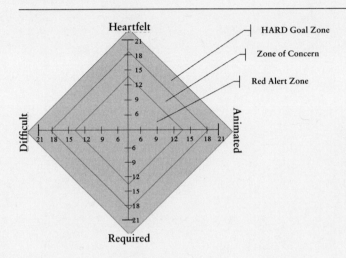

Get more examples and tools at hardgoals.com.

# 1

# Heartfelt

Whenever I talk to somebody about his or her goals—whether that person is trying to change the world, grow a company, or lose a few pounds—one of the first questions I ask is, "Why do you care about this goal?" (Don't worry, I'm not without some social graces; we actually have a conversation first.)

Some people look me right in the eye and say, "It doesn't mean anything to me. It's my boss/spouse/doctor and so forth who cares." I've lost count of the number of CEOs who've answered with, "Well, it's our Chairman who really feels this goal is important. . . ." And how many kids, when asked the same question, would answer, "It has nothing to do with me. I'm only doing it because my parents are making me"?

"Why do you care about this goal?" It's a simple question, and a frighteningly accurate way to predict whether or not somebody will abandon his or her goals at the slightest roadblock. The people who will pursue their goals regardless of the challenges will answer with something like, "This goal is my passion, it's what I'm here to do," or, "I love my children too much to not accomplish this," or even, "What I really care about is the finish line; I'm totally pumped to get to the payoff."

But when people say, "My boss/spouse/doctor/chairman is the one who really cares about this goal," or, "I'm doing it only because I have to," all signs point to the negative. It's right there in their words: these people lack any real emotional connection to their goals; the goals are not heartfelt. In fact, emotionally, such a goal is not even really that person's goal; it belongs to somebody else.

When you ask someone this question (and I encourage you to test it out for yourself), listen to the proper nouns and pronouns you get in response. If ownership of the goal is taken with a *me*, *mine*, *my*, or *I*, even though the goal may have originated with someone else, it's a strong sign that person will see that goal through to the end, no matter what gets thrown in the way.

But if the person mentally assigns ownership of the goal to a boss, spouse, doctor, chairman, or whomever, which you'll hear in words like *his*, *hers*, *the company's*, *my teacher*, or *the boss*, then you know the person is just not feeling connected to the goal. You can also listen for the emotional words that are said (for example, *pumped*, *excited*, *can't wait*, *fired up*, and so forth). Expressing intense feelings usually portends better results than emotional detachment does. Just remember, nobody ever washed a rental car (which means that if you don't own it, you're not going to put much effort into it).

You'd do just about anything for the people you love— your kids, spouse, best friend, family, significant other, and so forth—because you have a heartfelt connection to them. You don't just know these folks; you know you really care for them. But what if you were asked to do something for a passing acquaintance or even a total stranger? Most likely you'd exert some effort because you're a nice person, but most people would risk and sacrifice much more for a loved one than they would for an acquaintance or stranger. Doctors give more comprehensive care to people they feel more connected to. People give more money to charities when they feel a heartfelt connection to the recipients. Research has even shown that sales generated at Tupperware parties can be significantly explained by analyzing the strength of the personal connection between the host and the guests.

With all due respect to Sting, if you love somebody (and thus have a heartfelt connection to them), you're probably not going to set them free. Because of that heartfelt connection, you're going to follow them to the far corners of the globe, dripping blood, sweat, and tears to help them in any way you can. And that's precisely the kind of heartfelt connection you want to feel toward your goals. You want to love, need, and be deeply connected to your goals; you want to feel like you'd chase a goal to the very ends of the earth in order to fulfill it.

Just to be clear, it's not all about emotions. You absolutely need the analytical part of your brain to create and achieve a HARD Goal (as you'll clearly see in the "Required" and "Difficult" chapters). Certainly you should calculate the precise amount of weight you need to lose, the dollar amount by which your sales should grow, what mile mark you need to hit to be marathon ready, and how many classes you need to attend to experience the optimal level of challenge. But while you can create the most analytically sound goal in the world (with just the right degree of difficulty and so on), if it's not heartfelt, if you're not emotionally connected to it, if you aren't ready to chase this goal to the far corners of the globe, then you're more likely to abandon it than you are to accomplish it. Goal-setting processes often get so hung up on the analytical and tactical parts that they often neglect the most fundamental question: why do you care about this goal?

In the early days of my career, I advised seriously troubled organizations (the ones teetering on the edge of bankruptcy). And believe me when I say they needed some seriously HARD Goals to fight their way back. I could always tell if the company had a sufficient foundation from which to launch a successful turnaround just by walking around and asking employees, "Why do you care if this company succeeds or fails?" If I heard a lot of people say, "Because I'll lose my job," or "I need a paycheck," or something similar, I knew the company probably wouldn't make it. But if I heard something more heartfelt like, "I've poured my heart and soul into this place, and I'm not gonna let it fail now," or "Too many people are counting on us," or "Our customers need us to survive," then I knew we had a great shot at a comeback.

By the way, every politician that wants to survive knows that caring, emotional intensity, and heartfelt connection all mean the same thing: voter turnout. When people are emotionally connected to an issue or leader, when they feel heartfelt enthusiasm, they'll move heaven and earth to guarantee its success. But when they're apathetic—that's very bad news indeed!

If your goals are important enough, if they're HARD, then at some point you're going to hit a stumbling block, because every goal worth doing is going to test your resolve and ask you to decide if you really want to keep going. And at that moment, if your commitment to that goal is sufficiently heart-felt, you'll saddle up and plow right through. But if it's not, if there's no heartfelt connection, well, that's why your local gym is overcrowded with resolution makers in January and empty by March.

In the past few years there's been a spate of books on how to be happy. Not deeply fulfilled, emotionally resilient, high achieving, or doing something truly meaningful and significant with your life, but rather, happy. (Doing really easy stuff like gorging on pizza while drinking beer and watching *Blade Run-ner* would make me happy, but that's not exactly a recipe for self-respect or a life well-lived.) In one of these happiness books, the author tells a story about a woman who loved reading lit-erature so much that she decided to pursue her doctorate in the field. According to the story, the woman got into a good program and started taking classes. However, she quickly dis-covered that it was hard. There were grades, deadlines, papers, rewards, punishments, and so on. She eventually said, "I don't look forward to reading anymore."

Now, the author of the book was making a totally different point in telling this story, but here's what I took away from it: that woman didn't have a deep enough emotional connection to her goal; her connection wasn't truly heartfelt. Listen, just about every goal worth doing is going to take work. You don't just roll out of bed and get a Ph.D. because you enjoy reading Shake-speare. Were that the case, I'd win the Tour de France because I recently took a wine-drinking (er, I mean tasting) bike tour through Napa Valley. And maybe a Nobel Prize too because I love talking to smart people.

Once again, every goal worth doing will test your limits; there's simply no getting around it. And, at some point, even the things you love doing might stop being "fun" while you push yourself to hang on, keep going, to continue pushing and striving for a higher level of greatness. If the woman in that story truly cares about achieving her Ph.D. and becoming a professor of literature—which is a significant and meaningful accomplishment that will stay with her for the rest of her life—she's going to need a much deeper commitment than just, "Reading Shakespeare on the couch is fun."

So what do you do if you're not feeling as intensely plugged in as you'd like toward your goals? How do you build that emotional connection so that nothing short of death or disaster will get in your way of seeing those goals though?

There are three ways to build a heartfelt connection to your goals:

- **Intrinsic:** Develop a heartfelt connection to the goal itself.
- **Personal:** Develop a heartfelt connection to the person you're doing a goal for.
- **Extrinsic:** Develop a heartfelt connection to the payoff.

Let's look at each of these in more detail.

---

## INTRINSIC CONNECTION

You'll likely be more motivated to do something you really love doing. This is an insight that probably falls in the category of "well, duh" for most people. It's also, in a nutshell, the definition of intrinsic motivation. Consider what you do in your free time, when nobody's pressuring or rewarding you one way or another. Whatever it is, if it's something you love doing, it's probably an example of intrinsic motivation.

Steve Jobs has an intrinsic emotional connection to what he does. If you've ever listened to him launch a new product, the intrinsic connection positively oozes out of him. You can hear his heartfelt connection in statements like "This is an awesome computer," or "This is the coolest thing we've ever done with video," or "This is an incredible way to have fun." Jobs's passionate connection to the better world he truly believes he is creating with his products is what keeps all those great new ideas coming. It's also part of the package that turns Apple customers and employees into Apple evangelists.

Intrinsic motivation comes from the inside, not in response to external rewards. Not to say Jobs, or anyone playing off of intrinsic motivation, can't also seek external rewards. But the factor that drives the goal forward, the primary motivation, comes from doing what you love to do.

Coach, lecturer, and author Lyle Nelson is a four-time Olympian. In 1988 he was unanimously elected to serve as team captain of the United States Olympic Team. Pretty awesome stuff, though if you met him, you'd see only modesty and generosity. Lyle's always got a moment for anyone who asks, and since he's a terrific problem solver, he gets asked a lot.

When asked to describe how emotions played a part in his Olympic success, here's what Lyle had to say: "There I was in Innsbruck, Austria, the morning of my first race. The weather was perfect for skiing, cold and crisp, yet bright and sunny. I can still see the cross-country ski trails as they wandered along the lakeshore past a church spire and out of sight over the hill. That's when it dawned on me that I was about to live a dream."

"I thought back to when I was 15. I knew I'd get to the Olympics then, but I didn't know it would take 12 years to happen. Four of those years I was at West Point, and during my junior and senior years I lifted weights six nights a week from 11 P.M. to one in the morning. It was easy; it didn't take any Herculean discipline. I was powered by the thought of one day standing in the starting gate at the Olympics."[1]

Guided by a heartfelt intrinsic connection to his goal, Lyle made an unwavering commitment to becoming an Olympian when he was just a kid. That was a pretty heady ambition, but as Lyle goes on to say, it's not just about gigantic goals like becoming an Olympian. "As I stood in that gate, I realized that for the first time in my life I was going to try for a true 100 percent; no excuse for holding back would ever matter. It was one of those moments in life where we get to say to ourselves, 'When I step over this line I'm going to give it everything I have.' But that line could just as easily be a project at work, a relationship, or the resolve to change an attitude." Lyle's right, and giving 100 percent definitely comes easier when you have an intrinsic connection to your goal.

So how do you create an intrinsic heartfelt connection to your goals? By understanding your Shoves and Tugs.

Everybody has Shoves and Tugs. Shoves are those issues that demotivate you, drain your energy, stop you from giving 100 percent, and make you want to quit pursuing your goals (they "shove" you out the metaphorical door). Tugs are those issues that motivate and fulfill you, that you inherently love, that make you want to give 100 percent, and that keep you coming back no matter how hard things get. (They "tug" at you to keep pursuing your goal.)

This seems simple enough. But here's the twist: Shoves and Tugs are *not* flip sides of the same coin. Just because people are feeling serious Tugs toward their goals does *not* mean they don't have any Shoves. And before you spend all day trying to figure out how to get more Tugs into your goals, you've got to at least acknowledge (and ideally mitigate) the Shoves.

Let me begin with an analogy that's a little "out there," but it might help clarify this issue. Much like Shoves and Tugs are not opposites of each other, so too pain and pleasure are not opposites of each other. The flip side of pleasure isn't pain; it's just the absence of pleasure. Similarly, the antithesis of pain isn't pleasure; it's just the absence of pain. If somebody is hitting my foot with a hammer, that's pain. And when he or she stops, that's not pleasure, that's just no more pain. If I'm getting the world's greatest backrub, that's pleasure. When it stops, that's not pain, that's just no more pleasure.

Here's the lesson: If I'm getting a great backrub, it does not preclude somebody from starting to hit my foot with a hammer. And if that happens, the pain in my foot will totally detract from the pleasure I'm getting from the backrub. Here's a corollary lesson: If you walk past me one day and see that my foot is being hit with a hammer, you cannot fix the pain in my foot by giving me a backrub. The only way to stop the pain in my foot is to stop the hammer from hitting my foot.

I warned you that this is a weird analogy, but here's why it's relevant. Every day as people pursue their goals, their feet are being hit by hammers (Shoves). This quite effectively destroys any intrinsic attachment these folks might feel toward their goals. Worse yet, many people haven't consciously analyzed their Shoves and Tugs, so when they hit those Shoves they're not sure exactly why their heartfelt connection is waning, and they're even less sure how to address the problem.

So the first thing you have to do is diagnose your own Shoves and Tugs. And to do that, you just need to answer two simple questions:

- Describe a time recently (in the past few weeks or months, or even a year) when you felt really frustrated or emotionally burned out or like you wanted to chuck it all and give up.
- Describe a time recently (in the past few weeks or months, or even a year) when you felt really motivated or excited or like you were totally fired up and unstoppable.

You'll notice that these questions are not asked in the abstract. That's because I'm not looking for things that *might* derail my goals. I'm looking for the things that actually *are* derailing my goals (and the more recent your examples, the better). If I ask for a hypothetical list of what I "imagine" will derail my goals, I'll get a hypothetical list, and that's not exactly a whole lot of help. It's not typical behavior to abandon a goal because of a Shove that hasn't yet happened and might not ever happen. But lots of people will quit their goals because of a Shove they're experiencing this week.

Once you've discovered the kinds of factors and situations that add to or detract from your heartfelt connection to your goals, you can choose goals more suited to your intrinsic drives. People who are always looking for that next adrenaline rush might be Shoved by goals that aren't exciting or unique enough. People who love solving really tough problems might be getting Tugs from attempting a goal that their friends told them couldn't be achieved.

But what about the situations where you don't get to choose your goals? What if your goal has Shoves and you can't avoid them? In those cases you're going to need another level of motivation; you're going to need a Personal or Extrinsic connection to your goal.

Harvard economist Roland Fryer Jr. is doing something extraordinary—he's studying how to get inner-city kids more connected to the goal of succeeding in school. You may have heard of his latest study.[2] One of the largest studies regarding education policy ever undertaken, it involved using mostly private money to pay 18,000 kids a total of $6.3 million in various financial incentives in the classroom. The financial motivators used varied in amount and included payments for positive behaviors such as good grades, reading books, or not fighting.

It's a political hot potato, to say the least, but it underscores one critical issue: When you're having trouble building an intrinsic connection between a person and a goal, what else can you try? Sure, we all want kids to learn for the love of learning (in other words, to be intrinsically connected to the goal of academic success). But as Fryer says, "I could walk into a completely failing school, with crack vials on the ground outside, and say, 'Hey, I went to a school like this, and I want to help.' And people would just browbeat me about 'the love of learning,' and I would be like, 'But I just stepped on crack vials out there! There are fights in the hallways! We're beyond that."[3]

---

## PERSONAL CONNECTION

When I was a teenager, my great aunt Norma was diagnosed with terminal cancer. She was in her eighties at the time and had a warmth and charm that belied her underlying "mama bear" ferocity. Just after she was told she had a few months to live, her daughter (who was then in her sixties) was also diagnosed with cancer, but with a life expectancy closer to a few years. Of course, you know what I'm going to say next. Aunt Norma didn't pass right away; she lived for five more years. Her doctors were left scratching their heads with a combination of amazement and incredulity. Norma dealt with constant pain. But she fought through it every day so that she could care for her daughter.

We all know an Aunt Norma, someone who loves another person so much, is so emotionally connected to that person, that he or she can endure any pain—overcome any challenge—in order to help that person through a challenge or crisis. After you get past all the horror stories on your local news, you may find examples there. Like Nick Harris, the man from Ottawa, Kansas, who saw his six-year-old neighbor get run over by a car.[4]

The little girl was walking down her street on her way to school when someone backed out of a driveway and hit her, pushing her out into the street and rolling the car on top of her. Nick, who had just dropped his own daughter off at school, saw the accident and ran over to help. When he got there, this 5-foot-7, 185-pound guy lifted the car (a Mercury sedan) right off the little girl. And about her injuries? Some scrapes and bruises and road rash, but otherwise she's fine. Smiling, she told a local news team, "I didn't even break a bone."

There are loads of stories like this about people who have done something amazing to help another human being. The power to do so comes from a place of deep personal connection, because even if it's for a total stranger, there is still the human bond at work. It's what motivates so many people to get involved with or give to charities that have nothing to do with their own circumstances. Whether you're endeavoring to effect global humanitarian efforts or help a beloved family member or friend, you embrace taking on your HARD Goal for the benefit it will deliver to someone other than yourself.

Researchers at University College London used functional magnetic resonance imaging (fMRI) to demonstrate the neurological power possessed by deep attachments to other people[5] (fMRI measures the change in blood flow related to neural activity in the brain). Mothers were shown pictures of their own infants and then pictures of friends' kids, their best friend, and other adult friends, all the while measuring how their brains responded.

When they looked at their own kids, reward centers in the mothers' brains were activated coinciding with areas rich in oxytocin and vasopressin receptors (two neurohormones involved in maternal attachment and adult pair-bonding). Another area that's been linked to pain suppression during intense emotional experiences (like childbirth) was also activated. But perhaps even more interesting than the areas that were activated are the areas that became deactivated. The researchers found that areas associated with negative emotions, social judgments, and assessing other people's intentions were suppressed. And it wasn't just maternal love creating this effect; the same researchers looked at romantic love and found strikingly similar results.

A deep emotional connection to another person can be just the boost you need to override any negative thoughts and get your passions flowing for your HARD Goal. Not too shabby. Of course, if would be optimal if you only had to develop emotional connections to people you already know and love. However, were that the case, this would be nothing more than a schmaltzy collection of tearjerker stories—which it isn't.

Not everyone involved in or directly affected by your goal is going to be a personal favorite of yours, or even someone you actually know. But you can still develop a deep connection to almost any goal by becoming emotionally connected to the beneficiaries of that goal. The following techniques will work whether you're trying to lose weight because you want to live longer for your kids or because you want to impress an old high school squeeze at your upcoming reunion. If you want to accumulate more wealth for the financial security of your spouse or start an orphanage in Haiti. And also if you're CEO of Apple or Google and you want everyone in the world to be better off because they're using your products or you want to inspire employees to jump on a new sales initiative. They're all personal connections that can help you get where you want to go.

## Individualize

The first insight you need comes from my list of great women in history: Mother Teresa. Prefiguring a wealth of psychological and neurological research she said, "If I look at the mass I will never act. If I look at the one, I will." The genius in her statement is this: if you want to build a personal emotional connection to a goal, and give yourself that enormous motivational boost, individualize and personalize your goal.

One of the great psychologists of our time, the late Amos Tversky, conducted a study with Donald Redelmeier to see if physicians would recommend different treatments to patients if they thought about them as unique individuals rather than as anonymous members of a group of people with the same medical issues.[6] Physicians were given different medical scenarios and asked to choose the most appropriate treatment. There were two versions of each scenario: one described an individual patient, the other described a group of patients. Here's an example:

- **The individual perspective:** For example, H.B. is a young woman well known to her family physician and free from any serious illnesses. She contacts her family physician by phone because of five days of fever without any localizing symptoms. A tentative diagnosis of viral infection is made, symptomatic measures are prescribed, and she is told to stay "in touch." After about 36 hours she phones back reporting feeling about the same: no better, no worse, no new symptoms. The choice must be made between continuing to follow her a little longer by telephone or else telling her to come in now to be examined. Which management would you select for H.B.?

- **The group perspective:** For example, consider young women who are well known to their family physicians and free from any serious illnesses. They might contact their respective family physicians by phone because of five days of fever without any localizing symptoms. Frequently a tentative diagnosis of viral infection is made, symptomatic measures are prescribed, and they are told to stay "in touch." Suppose that after about 36 hours they phone back reporting feeling about the same: no better, no worse, no new symptoms. The choice must be made between continuing to follow them a little longer by telephone or else telling them to come in now to be examined. Which management strategy would you recommend?

Notice the difference. In the first scenario, you're thinking about H.B., an individual patient. In the second scenario, you're thinking about a group of patients.

These scenarios were given to doctors in a range of settings; some received the individual scenarios while others received the group scenarios. Now, here's the fascinating part: physicians who read the group scenarios recommended just sticking with phone follow-up anywhere from two to six times as often as those who read the individual scenario! Maybe it's just me, but I'd rather come in and see my doctor face-to-face.

In another scenario, physicians were asked whether to order an extra blood test to detect a rare but treatable condition for a college student presenting with fatigue, insomnia, and difficulty concentrating.[7] Depending on the kind of physician they asked (academic, county, and so forth), doctors who read the individual scenario recommended the extra test (even though it cost more money) anywhere from two to six times as often. Again, and maybe I'm weird here, I'd like the extra test to rule out the treatable blood condition.

So what can we learn? When they see somebody as an individual rather than as an anonymous member of a group, even highly analytical people like doctors respond differently. Which part would you rather play in these scenarios: the individual or the anonymous group member? (In my professional life, I'm a pretty well-known proponent of humanizing the doctor-patient relationship. And in my personal life, I'm just a guy who likes to know that my doctor is really paying attention to me as an individual and doing everything in his or her power to make me well. So I'm going to vote for being the "individual" in these cases.)

Now go back to what Mother Teresa said: "If I look at the mass I will never act. If I look at the one, I will." I'd say that lady was scary smart.

## Personalize

A group of researchers headed by Deborah Small at the Wharton School of the University of Pennsylvania essentially proved Mother Teresa's insight correct. In fact, their research paper begins with her quote. They designed a series of experiments to see whether people would donate more money to help an identifiable victim compared to a statistical victim.[8]

Each of the experiments had a few parts. First, participants completed an irrelevant marketing survey for which they were paid five one-dollar bills. Their pay was accompanied by a blank envelope and a charity request letter. (The marketing survey was just an excuse to get some money into the participants' hands to see if they could be induced to part with it.) The letter indicated they could donate any of their newly acquired five one-dollar bills to the charity Save the Children (which helps fight hunger in Africa).

In one of the experiments, three versions of the charity letter were distributed to three groups. The first group's letter gave statistics about hunger (the "statistical victim"). The statistical victim pitch went like this (this is just a brief excerpt):

> Food shortages in Malawi are affecting more than three million children. In Zambia, severe rainfall deficits have resulted in a 42 percent drop in maize production from 2000. As a result, an estimated three million Zambians face hunger . . .

The second group's letter gave a portrait of an identifiable victim. The individual victim pitch went like this (again, this is just an excerpt):

> Any money that you donate will go to Rokia, a seven-year-old girl from Mali, Africa. Rokia is desperately poor, and faces a threat of severe hunger or even starvation. Her life will be changed for the better as a result of your financial gift . . .

The third group got a letter that gave them both; they got pieces of the statistical victim pitch followed by the identifiable victim pitch.

Out of the possible $5, people who read the statistical victim pitch gave an average of $1.14. People who got the combined pitch (statistical and identifiable victim) gave $1.43. And people who read just the identifiable victim pitch? They gave $2.38. Yes, you read that right. People who only read about Rokia, who could personalize the person they were helping, gave more than twice as much money as those who were only giving to help a statistic.

A follow-up experiment was conducted with the same statistical and identifiable victim scenarios. However, this time participants were "primed" to think in a particular way. One group was primed for thinking "analytically" by asking them questions like, "If an object travels at five feet per minute, then, by your calculations, how many feet will it travel in 360 seconds?" The other group was primed for "feeling" with questions like "When you hear the word *baby*, what do you feel?"

Here's the kicker: When people were primed to "feel" before reading about Rokia, they gave $2.34, about the same as they did without being primed. But when they were primed to "analyze" before reading about Rokia, they only gave $1.19. They gave almost 50 percent less just by engaging the analytical part of their brain instead of the feeling part of their brain.

Now, let me offer a giant "holy mackerel" moment for business leaders whose job it is to set goals for their team. You know how corporations like things that are measurable? And how they're always asking employees to translate big fuzzy goals into a simple number that's easily trackable? Well, whenever employees are asked to translate goals they might "feel" good about, have an emotional connection to, into a simple number that "analytically" fits their spreadsheet, you may have just cut their willingness to "give" to that goal by 50 percent.

You want your employees to dig deep into their emotional bank account and give, give, give toward big corporate goals. Asking them to "analyze" the goal long before you instigate any kind of talk about "feeling" the goal is not the way to get there. In fact, some companies go so far as to denigrate the feelings and elevate the "number" to some deified position ("Ahhh, I saw the number and it was goooood," "The number shall set you free").

Here's a line from a recent *Businessweek* article that should serve as a cautionary tale for every business executive: "Not too long ago, GM executives wore buttons bearing the numeral '29' as a constant reminder of the company's lofty goal of 29 percent U.S. market share."[9] As I write this book, that number is around 19 percent. I feel like asking, "Soooo, how's that number-on-a-button thing working out for ya?"

I'm not saying you don't need numbers (I like numbers—I'm a researcher at heart, and I've won awards for number-driven studies on numerical topics like financial management). But boy do you have to be careful about killing off people's feelings toward their goals when you're at the beginning of the goal-setting process. Some companies still use a fairly antiquated goal-setting process called SMART Goals (which stands for Specific, Measurable, Achievable, Realistic, and Time-Limited). Not only do you not see the words *feel* or *heartfelt* anywhere in there, but Specific and Measurable are the pieces that usually get companies all excited about turning every goal into a number (ironically killing off any real excitement that might have existed).

Later on in the book I'll show you how to effectively integrate numbers into your goals. But for now, suffice it to say that numbers come after feelings. If you're trying to lose 20 pounds, until you have a deep emotional connection to that goal, don't go making any buttons with "20" on them. The same goes for posting "20" sticky notes on the bathroom mirror or the refrigerator—at least if you care about keeping your goal alive.

When you're at the beginning of your goal process, you need to develop feeling. You want an emotional attachment to your goals that gives you the ceaseless energy to pursue them no matter how tough it gets. Otherwise you too will have big buttons with numbers that are nothing more than a reminder of a failed goal that you weren't all that emotionally attached to in the first place.

## Apple Versus Microsoft: A Perfect Example of Individualizing and Personalizing

Do you remember those "I'm a Mac, I'm a PC" ads that Apple ran (and may still be running, depending on when you're reading this book)? Against a plain white background, a hip casual guy (played by Justin Long) introduces himself as a Mac ("Hello, I'm a Mac."). And then John Hodgman, playing the totally un-hip caricature of a spreadsheet-addicted data nerd (in a brown-ish suit that wasn't particularly well tailored), says, "And I'm a PC." Then they have some interaction in which they debate the merits of a Mac versus a PC (gee, guess who wins?).

Here's an example:

MAC: iLife comes on every Mac.
PC: iLife, well, I have some very cool apps that are
    bundled with me.
MAC: Like, what have you got?
PC: Calculator.
MAC: That's cool. Anything else?
PC: Clock.

OK, I know, this is way funnier when you actually see the com-mercial; but you get the idea. What's the point of these com-mercials? To individualize and personalize. Apple wants to put a name and a face on Macs and PCs because that's where they'll get your emotional connection. And while the ads are hysteri-cal, they did make one mistake: the guy playing the PC is comic gold. John Hodgman is superbly talented, he gets the best laugh lines, and he's funny while still engendering some sympathy. So while Apple wants you emotionally bonded to the Mac, and the ads accomplish that, you also end up emotionally connected to the PC because the actor's so good.

How did Microsoft fight these ads? By doing a complete 180 away from the normal hyperanalytical Microsoft stereotype.

They launched the "I'm a PC" ads showing real people fighting against the stereotype that Apple reinforced. These people include farmers, techies, brides, and scuba divers saying things like, "I'm a PC," "I don't wear a suit," "I wear headbands," and so on. The whole point of these ads was to individualize and personalize—just like the Apple ads.

Microsoft learned its lesson well. When the company unveiled Windows 7, its ads were built on the theme "Windows 7 Was My Idea." These ads showed normal people talking up the features of Windows 7 while basically saying, "These features were my idea." So if Apple ever tries to attack those features, who are they attacking? Those normal, nice, regular people. It's one thing to attack a nameless, faceless corporation, or even a cartoonish stereotype, but are you really going to attack some kid or mom or dad who essentially says, "I'm that PC, and when you attack *it*, you attack *me*!" I don't think so.

## Great Companies Build Personal Connections

Every so often I hear someone say, "This emotional connection stuff is fine for losing weight or quitting smoking, but it'll never work for business goals." OK, I hear your concern. But, not to put too fine a point on it, you're wrong. And let me show you why.

There's nothing inherently implausible about a CEO rolling out of bed in the morning, intrinsically motivated to go to the office and create shareholder wealth. And when one of his kids asks, "Will you be home in time for my soccer game tonight, Daddy?" the CEO could sincerely apologize and say, "I'm sorry, little Billy, but thousands of people are counting on me to finish this report so their stock goes up and they have enough money to buy food and clothes."

Now, imagine the guy who works the line at that organization skipping into the office to create shareholder wealth. Or saying to his little Billy, "I'm sorry, son, but Daddy has to weld three more parts so the company's stock price goes up by a millionth of a point, thus making some rich people just a little richer. And no, we won't see even a dime of it, so don't ask for that new bike."

Money is great, and it's absolutely necessary, but working for money will always be an inadequate motivator if there isn't also something more emotional. They're not mutually exclusive, of course, but too many companies act as if once they've offered employees some money, they've finished with the task of connecting people to their goals. A few senior executives may be intrinsically charged up to boost share price, but the folks on the frontlines need something else, too. And frankly, companies whose sole existential anchor is money (for example, Enron, Bear Stearns, Lehman Brothers) will never outperform a company whose existence is predicated on creating an emotional attachment to customers.

If you're the CEO of a company, I'd be willing to bet that Google makes more money than your organization. That's not a slight, just a (likely) statement of fact. (By my quick calculations, at the end of 2009 Google had over $26 billion in working capital.) And yet, when it comes to setting goals, Googlers are all about personal emotional connection.

Serving something more emotional than money is really hard for a lot of companies. Google says it very well in its corporate philosophy, which includes a list of "Ten things we know to be true."[10] Here's number one on that list:

**1. Focus on the user and all else will follow.**
   *While many companies claim to put their customers first, few are able to resist the temptation to make small sacrifices to increase shareholder value.* From its inception, Google has steadfastly refused to make any change that does not offer a benefit to the users who come to the site:

> The interface is clear and simple.
> Pages load instantly.
> Placement in search results is never sold to anyone.
> Advertising on the site must offer relevant content and not
>   be a distraction.

The italicizing above is mine, and it's to make a point. Every company on earth puts the word *customer* or *patient* or *user* in its mission statement. It looks great embossed on a plaque hanging in the boardroom or lobby, but are we actually willing to put it into our goals? Would we make sacrifices to serve that customer, patient, user, or whoever we state as our higher purpose?

Companies that tend to make the most money over time do so by delivering the most value to somebody they consider bigger than themselves, not by sacrificing the customer to immediately increase shareholder value. Sure, you can pop your stock for a quarter here or there through financial narcissism, but it will eventually come back to bite you. Not only will your customers eventually revolt, but your best employees won't give

100 percent to a self-serving cause. And your best employees might even quit you to go work at Google.

---

## EXTRINSIC CONNECTION

Let's say you've exhausted your options for developing an intrinsic or personal connection to your goals. Or you've got both intrinsic and personal connections to your goal, but you still need something more. Are there any other options? Well, if you remember Roland Fryer, the Harvard economist studying whether financial incentives will motivate kids to learn even when there are crack vials on the front steps of the school, you need to find something, anything, to get you motivated. And the emotional connectivity that arises when you desperately want the payoff that comes at the end of a goal isn't as lame as some critics make it out to be. Yes, you should exhaust every attempt to find an intrinsic or personal connection, and not make financial rewards your only, or default, option (Google and others showed why this is true). But extrinsic rewards do have their place, and if used effectively, they can help get you started.

There are those folks who will argue against extrinsic rewards, and even go as far as to say they can hurt your commitment to a goal. Take, for example, a study done in Washington State of 1,200-plus people who were trying to quit smoking.[11] One subgroup of study participants was offered a financial incentive to use some smoking cessation self-help materials. What was found was that the financial incentive got people to use the self-help materials, but because it supposedly undermined their intrinsic motivation to quit, the incentive did not actually increase their smoking cessation rates and they had higher relapse rates.

Read that and you might be inclined to think rewards like money kill off any real motivation. Not so. You see, one of the big questions we have to ask in a study like this is, what were the actual financial incentives? Because when we do, we find out that first there was the reward of a ceramic coffee mug. And second, there were drawings whereby study participants had some statistical possibility of winning a trip to Hawaii, the San Juan Islands, or downtown Seattle.

As a former smoker, let me offer a commentary on these "financial incentives." First, that coffee mug could have been delivered with candy and a stripper and it wouldn't have gotten anywhere near motivating me to quit smoking. Heck, given the number of swag coffee mugs I've got around the house, I'd probably be willing to pay the researchers to keep the darn thing. It's practically a disincentive to quit. And by the way, the only thing better than a cigarette, is a cigarette with coffee. So that's a really good subliminal reminder to smoke. Jeez, why didn't they just send a lighter and a pack of Marlboros?

And the raffle for a trip to Hawaii? If those study participants were even a little mathematically inclined, they'd guess the retail price of the trip at $3,000 (just to pick a round number), then they'd say, "My odds of winning are 1 in 300 (0.3%)" or whatever, and then they'd discover that the trip has an expected monetary value of about $10 ($3,000 × 0.3% = $10). Without some deeper emotional connection, no smoker on earth will be motivated to quit by offering him or her $10 and a coffee mug reminder to smoke more.

A different study, reported in *The New England Journal of Medicine*, that was a bit more astute on the use of financial motivators, found that incentives *do* work.[12] Half the people in the study were offered information about smoking cessation programs. The other half were offered the information plus a financial incentive. The financial incentives were $100 for completing a smoking cessation program, another $250 for quitting smoking within 6 months after enrolling in the study, and another $400 for staying provably smoke free 6 months later. (Smoking abstinence was measured with a simple biochemical test for cotinine.)

So, was $750 better than $10? Well, let's see. The people who got the financial incentives had a 294 percent higher smoking cessation rate than the information-only group 9 or 12 months after enrolling in the study. The incentive group also had a 261 percent higher smoking cessation rate than the information-only group 15 or 18 months after enrolling in the study. And, of course, they had almost triple the rates of enrollment in smoking cessation programs, over quadruple the completion rates, and almost double the smoking cessation rates within the first 6 months. So I'm going to say yes, the extrinsic rewards worked.

Extrinsic connections do work. Again, in an ideal world, you want an intrinsic and/or a personal connection. But when you've exhausted those, or you still need a little something extra, extrinsic connections are available. What seems to be the real issue here is what kinds of extrinsic incentives work. An emerging school of thought, led by Columbia University professor E. Tory Higgins, is the notion of *regulatory fit*.[13] This basically means that the incentive has to be consistent with (or "fit") the way people think about their goal.

In a series of experiments, Higgins and his colleagues asked people to play a game called Shoot the Moon. A skill-oriented game from the 1940s, it involves rolling a small metal ball, the size of a marble, uphill by manipulating two metal rails. The goal is to separate the bars at just the right moment so the ball drops into the hole that carries the most points. (You can check it out on YouTube by searching for "shoot the moon game"; it's actually a pretty addictive little game.)

In one experiment, researchers told folks to just have fun playing the game because they were studying what types of games people found the most entertaining. Then they offered people a reward—a pen—for winning, but they varied the framing of the reward. One group had the reward described in serious tones, as if it were a work-related task, and with serious scoring on a whiteboard. The other group had the reward described in fun tones—imagine this is a carnival game where you can win a prize—and scoring was done with poker chips. Following all this they gave the participants some free time and covertly assessed how many in each group continued to play the game, and how many went on to other things like reading a magazine or playing computer games.

The results were fascinating. When people got the fun reward, it "fit" with the inherently fun activity. And thus, they continued to play the game more during their free period. (Watching what you do in your free time is a pretty good measure of what you find intrinsically motivating.) And when people got the serious reward, which did not fit at all with the fun activity, their intrinsic desire to play the game dropped. Nearly 71 percent of the people in the fun reward group played the game in the free period, compared to only 44 percent in the serious reward group.

Another of their experiments replaced playing Shoot the Moon with a serious task (financial duties) that was explained in a serious manner, not as a game, but rather as preparation for significant lifetime experiences. As in the earlier experiment, participants were informed in two different ways about a potential performance reward (once again, a pen): one framed in a serious approach and the other framed as enjoyable or fun.

Guess what? To a significant degree, the participants who had been told about the reward in a serious manner voluntarily chose to repeat the serious financial task when given a choice of what to do during their free time. Just as with the fun game and the fun reward, the serious reward was a better fit for the serious activity.

Here's the bottom line: rewards have to fit the activity. I've seen companies survive difficult times by asking their employees to sacrifice, work harder, and so forth. Tough, serious business. But then I've seen some of those same companies pass through their tough times and throw a company picnic to celebrate their survival. Sadly, sometimes those celebrations fail miserably. Why? Because the fun reward just doesn't fit the serious activity. The same goes for nonwork situations.

---

## INTRINSIC OR EXTRINSIC MOTIVATION: WHICH IS BEST?

Before I attempt to answer the question of which type of motivation is best, here's an example that shows the distinction between intrinsic and extrinsic behaviors. My wife truly enjoys running; she likes the relaxation, the runner's high, all of it.

For her, running is an intrinsically motivated activity. Not so in my case—and yet, I run. I don't inherently enjoy running: it's hard for me, it's painful, my head pounds, and I'm slow. I do it for health reasons, and frankly, because of the T-shirts I get at races (of course, those T-shirts make possible another extrinsic motivator, namely feeling cool when people ask me about the race). The "why" behind my running is a perfect example of extrinsic motivation. My wife and I have each run a marathon, but for very different reasons.

There are those who will say that intrinsic motivation is way better than extrinsic motivation. And some will take it even further and say that extrinsic motivation can actually hurt intrinsic motivation. One of the classic studies on this was called "Turning Play into Work."[14]

Researchers studied nursery school children who drew with felt pens—what you might call an intrinsically motivating activity. The kids were divided into three groups. The first was the expected reward condition, in which the kids agreed to draw a picture in order to receive a good player certificate. The second was the unexpected reward condition, in which participants were unexpectedly given a reward after they completed the picture. In the third, control condition, the children didn't receive any reward, they just got to draw.

One week later, all the kids were brought back in to play with the felt pens, and no rewards were given to any of the groups. The results? Kids in the expected reward group decreased in intrinsic motivation, while the other two groups maintained their intrinsic motivation.

OK, so perhaps if you give a lousy reward that's inconsistent with the activity itself, one that incents the wrong behaviors and diminishes someone's sense of autonomy, then yes, you can mess up that person's motivation. But does that mean extrinsic rewards are bad? Of course not. I could easily design a reward that would motivate whatever behavior I wanted. For starters, if my desired goal was that I wanted kids to be happy or creative while drawing, I'd probably give them a happy or creative reward, not a "good player certificate," which is neither happy nor creative.

But all of that is still very academic, and it misses two important points. First, in the real world, it's often tough to neatly separate intrinsic and extrinsic motivation. Consider, for example, a study in which participants completed an assessment that measured their intrinsic or extrinsic motivation. It was found that these two factors moderately correlate with each other. Remember your intro stats class when the professor said, "Any correlation over 0.3 is a moderately large correlation"? Well, in this particular study intrinsic and extrinsic motivation were correlated at 0.4. This means that intrinsic and extrinsic motivations were not diametrically opposed, nor even neatly compartmentalized; in fact, they were moderately related.

But you know what? Even if you could neatly separate intrinsic from extrinsic motivation, you might find another problem. Sometimes, even if you love doing something, the circumstances will change and doing that something will no longer be inherently enjoyable. Remember the woman who no longer loved reading literature because her Ph.D. program was so difficult? Well, what's the answer here? Stop the doctoral program? Just give up?

In a few years, what do you think will be more intrinsically rewarding to her: Being a quitter and maybe going back to reading Shakespeare on her couch by herself? Or finding a new source of motivation, a deeper emotional connection to her goal than just "reading is fun" to push herself through the tough times of the doctoral program, to achieve her Ph.D. and ultimately become a professor of literature? Seriously, which path do you think offers her the greatest objective accomplishment (doing real things) and subjective accomplishment (feeling a deep sense of fulfillment)?

I am not intrinsically motivated to do any of the following: eat more vegetables, not smoke, exercise, save money, run, or grow a company (while simultaneously trying to eat healthy, exercise, and not smoke). In fact, it's only because I am so emotionally connected to the extrinsic "payoffs" from those activities that I do them at all. For example, eating healthy foods, exercising, and not smoking will give me a longer life with my wife and kids.

So what would I do if I were truly left to my own devices? Here's a list I made:

- Make love to my wife.
- Try to find a way to clone my wife to make item 1 even more fun.
- Play with my kids. (See? Item 1 wasn't frivolous, it was totally necessary to get me my kids. But yes, item 2 is just frivolous.)
- Eat Buffalo-style pizza. (Everyone thinks of Buffalo's wings, but for those of us who grew up there, the pizza is just as good.)
- Sit on the beach. (Trust me, if you grew up in Buffalo, you too would have an intrinsic drive for warmth and sand.)
- A whole bunch of other stuff that's completely unrelated to work.

- Research, writing about research, and talking about writing or research (the information that went into this book, our HARD Goals project, employee surveys, leadership assessments, and so on).

"You mean you don't intrinsically love being CEO of your own company and pushing it to grow bigger and bigger?" (you inquire as you gasp in horror). The answer is, I like it well enough, and I'm pretty good at it. However, I mostly do it because it allows me to create a job for myself where I get to do the research (and writing and talking about it). I love the world of ideas. I'm less intrinsically excited with the world of contracts, budgets, production meetings, invoices, IT security, and so on. Managing a company on a daily basis is for me the same thing as eating vegetables (not that I'm particularly skilled at eating vegetables, but it's a tolerable means to a much better end). Running is also in that category for me, as is financial management and a whole bunch of other stuff.

Now, here's something really interesting. I do the daily management stuff because I can make a contribution that leads to better results, and ultimately frees up more time for me to do more intrinsically motivated work, like writing books. Sometimes your extrinsic payoff can actually be more work, but intrinsically driven work. Do you know about Google's "20-percent time"? It's a workday per week when developers can choose projects that aren't necessarily in their job descriptions. They can use the time to develop something new, fix something broken, or create Google's next cool thing. Here's how Google describes it: "We offer our engineers "20-percent time" so that they're free to work on what they're really passionate about. Google Suggest, AdSense for Content and Orkut are among the many products of this perk."[15] Notice how it's basically an extrinsic payoff of working for them that takes the form of intrinsically motivated work. Can you see why Google is able to passionately set, pursue, and achieve such amazingly HARD Goals? And generate such tremendous financial returns?

---

## YOU CAN HAVE YOUR CAKE AND EAT IT TOO

Diana Sproveri was a talented screenwriter. After growing up on the East Coast and doing the New York writer scene for a while, she decided to move to Hollywood and give screenwriting a go. As I said, she's got talent, so it wasn't long before she was getting work. In fact, a while back, I sat with her on the set of the Nickelodeon show "True Jackson, VP" while they were filming the episode she wrote (tween television isn't really my bag, but I've got to admit, it was pretty funny). But as good a writer as she is, her connection to screenwriting wasn't heartfelt. A lesson for us all is to understand that being good at something is *not* the same as loving it. And so Diana sat herself down to assess her Shoves and Tugs.

When she made herself describe a time when she recently felt totally "on fire" and unstoppable, she surprised herself with her answer. During her son's naps and after his bedtime, she had been fiddling with her family's cake and cookie recipes. She'd always loved baking, but lately she'd really been taking it to a new level—trying to keep the extraordinary old-world flavors but adding the presentation of great art and in a form that would actually work for parties. Sounds simple enough, but she says, "I would take my mother's and grandmother's recipes, but to get them beautiful and extravagant enough for parties, while balancing the flavors and making them truly gourmet, I would have to doctor them up 30 or 40 times before I got them just the way I wanted."

The more she thought about it, the more she realized she would be a lot more fulfilled making cakes than writing sitcoms. And so she took the leap. She said, "I knew in my heart, notwithstanding the riskiness of this goal, that I could be '*the*' person that people thought of when they wanted special desserts for an event. I knew that I was going to be doing this on my own, because I had no budget to hire any help, so any event that I booked was going to be just me, all day and night. And while that might sound scary, it felt so right in my heart that I just had to try."

Diana's plan was successful. She started bringing her baked treats, artfully presented and made with all the love in her heart, to friends who worked at Hollywood studios. People began tasting the goodies, and word spread like wildfire. I can personally attest to this—she makes these treats which are bites of cake covered in chocolate and put on a stick, like a large lollipop made of cake. *Hollywood Today* described them a bit more elegantly when it reviewed them, saying, "A new category of dessert treat, these gourmet cake pops have the right amount of cake with a hard shell frosting. The very moist cake bites are covered with a layer of dark chocolate or white chocolate then decorated."[16] However you want to describe them, these delicious confections have all the flavor of the best cake you've ever eaten, but put on a lollipop stick. Not only are they fun, but you can delight your mouth and still look beautiful, like at the swank Grammy party Diana catered.

Of course, trying to launch a business around children's naps and evening hours is utterly exhausting. And so Diana gave herself extrinsic motivators for every event she booked, like buying the coolest kitchen gadgets or adding more elements to her desserts' presentations. Driven by her heartfelt connection to her work (intrinsic, extrinsic, and personal), people booked Diana, and her cupcakes, cookies, cakes, and more, for dessert tables at shows and events. In a town that's almost impossible to impress, Diana's used her heartfelt HARD Goal to invent the dessert party. While everybody else is trying to streamline to make their own lives easier (not exactly a HARD Goal), Diana's creating entire events based on desserts and a savory cheese course.

Did her heartfelt connection work? Well, she's been written up in *People* magazine, *Everyday with Rachael Ray*, *Sunset* magazine, and *Hollywood Today*, among others. Diana catered a party at the Grammys and provided treats for gift baskets at the Oscars. And her treats have become so sought after that she's looking into expansion. It's a really bad pun, but I'm pretty much obligated to deliver it: when you build a heartfelt connection to your goals, you'll find, as Diana did, that it gets a lot easier to have your cake and eat it too.

## SUMMARY

No one is more qualified to determine your most powerful emotional connection to your goal than you. Your doctor may have told you it's do or die when it comes to losing that 50 pounds, but what's your real reason for doing it? Maybe you really do just want to live longer. Or maybe it's the vision of your kids, or your grandkids that you haven't met yet, that keeps you from gorging on your particular food weakness. Or maybe someone, a spouse or parent, offered you $100 for every 10 pounds you lose as an incentive.

None of these motivators are wrong or right, as long as you plug in and make them work for you. So before you start thinking about all the things you're going to have to do to bring about your goal, take some time to answer the question I opened the chapter with: Why do you care about this goal? Is it something you just love to do, or are you doing it for someone else, for something bigger than yourself? Or are you really just after the payoff? Whatever your answer, if you can build a heartfelt connection to your goal, own that goal, and integrate it into your life, you're on your way to HARD Goal achievement.

Goals for which you have a heartfelt attachment add a dimension of "wanting" to achieve this goal instead of just "needing" to do it. While necessity is critical, this additional emotional connection makes a huge difference in how you approach your goal and the energy you devote to seeing it through. The exact mix of intrinsic, personal, and/or extrinsic motivators depends on your unique situation, as long as you assemble enough of them to build a deep connection. Because if you don't care about your goal, what's going to motivate you to try and achieve it? And if you don't care about your goal, how can you expect anyone whose help you need to make it happen (employees, spouse, or whoever) to care about it either?

Get more examples and tools at hardgoals.com.

# 2

## Animated

Seeing is believing. Do you get the picture? Can you see what I'm saying? Have I shed some light on the subject? We humans are visual creatures, and we respond to imagery. In fact, we're so visually oriented that even our language is filled with visual words like *seeing*, *picture*, *see*, and *light*. It doesn't matter if those images are on paper or a screen in front of us or just in our mind. If we can imagine something, see it, or picture it, we're a lot more likely to process, understand, and embrace it.

You could flood my ears with words for an hour, and I'd probably retain some of what you said, but show me a picture or help me to imagine what you're talking about, and you could probably save yourself 500 or 600 of those words. Even more impressive is that after seeing that picture or mental imagery, I'll remember a lot more of your message. Wait, what's that you say? A picture could replace more words than that? How many words could a picture replace—700, 800, 900? No way, you're telling me a picture is worth 1,000 words? (Whatever you do, don't tell my publisher. Otherwise they might drop me and just buy some stock photography.)

All jokes aside, the technical term is "pictorial superiority effect." It expresses the idea that concepts are much more likely to be remembered if presented as pictures rather than as words. To what extent do we remember more? Well, when we hear only information, our total recall is about 10 percent when tested 72 hours later. But add a picture, and that number shoots up to 65 percent.[1] It's a pretty substantial difference.

Every goal you're considering right now is competing for some finite resources: time, energy, attention, memory, and so forth. An individual—or a company or a country—can only pursue so many goals at one time. So some goals will get picked and pursued, while others get dropped like litter on our brains' highways. And one of the key determinants of whether or not we choose a goal for pursuit is how clearly and vividly we can picture that goal in our minds.

When it comes to motivating ourselves or others to achieve big goals, whoever has the best imagery wins. If your goal is to lose 30 pounds and you've got a vibrant and detailed picture of how great you'll look in those skinny jeans seared into your brain, an image so vivid you see it in your mind's eye every time you open the fridge, you'll probably stick to your diet and achieve your goal. But if you just can't picture it—you want to lose the weight, but you just can't visualize yourself dieting or exercising or being skinnier—then it's more than likely that your goal will remain unrealized.

Imagine your goal is to double the size of your company. If it's easier for your employees to picture the company staying the same size than it is for them to imagine how great the company would be 200 percent bigger, they'll never accept your goal (and probably drag their feet every step of the way). If you've ever heard somebody say, "I just don't see myself doing that," what you really heard was a guarantee that he or she will never willingly do whatever it is.

Let's have a little fun and try to save the world from colorlessness. Imagine you have scientific evidence that the planet is losing color and will soon turn completely black and white (like an old television set). Let's also say that remote places on earth are already losing color, that the occurrence of rainbows is down by 40 percent, and that you have mathematically sound projections that all color will be gone from the world within 10 years. Finally, imagine that you've discovered that the cause of the color loss is food coloring. With all the artificial food-like substances that people eat nowadays, the toxic-looking colors (such as fluorescent orange cheese and neon blue raspberry flavoring) are sucking up all of our colors.

So now, as an aspiring world influencer, you're going to set a HARD Goal. First, you need to convince all the people in the world that we're losing our color, and second, you need to convince them that in order to reverse the color loss, everyone needs to stop eating foods with artificial coloring.

That's a pretty difficult goal right there: convincing people of the need to change and then actually getting them to execute the change. And what will be your biggest impediment to this? Believe it or not, the hardest part won't be getting people to stop eating artificial cheese; it's going to be convincing them that the world is losing its color in the first place. (I'll cover this in the "Required" chapter, but if you were convinced that eating artificial cheese would kill you, you'd stop eating it without a struggle. However, if you had little to no buy-in to the dangers of artificial cheese, you'd probably keep eating it.) How do you get people to take you seriously when you say the world is losing its color? I mean, just look around your room or take a look outside; do you see colors? Go eat an apple or a strawberry; are they red? What color is the sky? The grass? Your car?

The biggest impediment you face in convincing people that the world is losing its color is that everyone can see colors all around them. You're trying to create a HARD Goal to convince people that the world is losing its colors, but your visuals stink. People can barely remember black-and-white television, let alone picture the whole world turning black and white. And if your "pitch" is built around scientific words and formulas, that's just not terribly compelling imagery. By contrast, the competing goal of denial—do nothing and keep eating fluorescent food—has great imagery; there are colors everywhere people look. Science is on your side. Health is on your side. So are logic, quality of life, doing what's right, and more. But imagery is not on your side, and as you'll learn in this chapter, visuals are essential. And thus, unless you make some serious improvements to your imagery, there are lots of people that won't be motivated to achieve this HARD Goal. The world will go solidly black and white before anyone plugs in to what you were trying to say.

This chapter is called "Animated," but there are all sorts of words to describe the process covered here: *picturing, visualizing, envisioning, imagining,* and many others. I chose the word *animate* because, well, admittedly, it fits the acronym *HARD* perfectly. But aside from that obvious fact, it really is the best word for the job. "Inspire, heighten, intensify, give lifelike qualities to," are all definitions of *animate*. And that's exactly what you're going to do to your goals.

A necessary part of making your goal compelling—so motivating, inspiring, and necessary that you'd move heaven and earth to achieve it—is making your goal imaginable. The more you can picture your goal, even if only in a drawing or a dream, the more real it becomes. And the more real a goal is, the more possible it is and the more you can conceive of it being a part of your life. Thus, it becomes a goal you'll do almost anything to achieve.

Stimulating the visual parts of your brain has a profound impact on your consciousness. Just look at how many people get freaked out about asteroids crashing into the planet after they see it happen on a movie screen. Or how about all the 5'7" Italian guys who thought they could become heavyweight boxers after watching *Rocky*? In fact, I'm still pretty much convinced his fight with Ivan Drago in *Rocky IV* ended the Cold War ("if I can change, and you can change, everybody can change").

I don't want to give some cliché like "if you can picture it, you can do it," because that's an oversimplification. Instead, let's say that the more you can picture a goal, the more intensely it will be encoded in your brain and the more it will insinuate itself into your life and consciousness, thus making the achievement of that goal a virtual necessity.

## PICTURE SUPERIORITY

There are lots of ways to animate a goal—to help you imagine, envision, and picture what you ultimately want to create and how you'll get there. You can use actual pictures, drawings, visualization, mnemonics, and even language filled with imagery. Of course, any opportunity you have to use a true visual (picture, drawing, or other image), go ahead and use it because these are incredibly powerful motivators.

Let me offer a graphic (pun intended) example of this. Researchers at Michigan State's medical school looked at 234 emergency room patients suffering from lacerations.[2] Following treatment, but before discharge, all patients were given home-care wound instructions. Half the patients were given text-only instructions, while the other half were given the text plus pictures (cartoons illustrating keys points from the text). Three days later researchers phoned the patients and inquired about the success of their care at home.

Here are the statistical highlights from those calls. First, patients who received the cartoons had a lot better recall of the information given in the instructions than the text-only group did. When quizzed, 46 percent of the people who got the picture-based instructions answered all four wound-care questions correctly, compared with only 6 percent of the people who got the text-only instructions. Additionally, the patients who got the pictures had 43 percent better actual adherence to those wound-care instructions than the text-only crowd. And, no big surprise here, 24 percent more of the picture crowd had actually read the instructions in the first place.

I know this is a book about goals, but pictures will truly help you sear anything into your brain—even something as mundane as remembering your computer passwords. A study conducted in California looked at computer password recall.[3] Most people pick really terrible passwords for their online accounts. In way too many cases, if you know even a little bit about a person you can guess his or her passwords. For instance, say you have a friend, Bob, who really likes wine. It might only take you a few tries to uncover his password, "merlot." But how easily would you arrive at "S@uvignon9823"?

Obviously, the latter is the better choice. Only Bob is not only more likely to use the former, he'll probably also use it on every one of his accounts (e-mail, credit cards, banking, Facebook, and so forth).

Researchers in this study looked at a few different ways of helping people develop and remember more complex, secure passwords. Study subjects were asked to develop a number of better passwords (they had to be at least eight characters in length and have at least an uppercase and lowercase letter, a digit, and a special character). This type of password might seem difficult to remember, but subjects were also given memory-assisting tools including image-based and text-based mnemonic techniques.

For the image-based mnemonics, subjects were taught how to look at a picture, pull out personal details, and turn those details into a password. For example, a woman with a picture of her boyfriend might look at it and say, "I date Matt." From there she can create a password such as EyeD8M@tt. That's a pretty uncrackable password that would also be really easy for her to remember (unless, of course, she dumps Matt anytime soon).

You can probably already guess where this is headed. The image-based mnemonic group significantly outperformed the text-based mnemonic group. Their passwords were more complex, and thus less crackable, and whether after 10 minutes or a week, they took less time to remember their passwords. They also needed fewer attempts to remember them and had fewer forgotten passwords.

So what do we need to know here? Basically that animation—imagery, visuals, pictures, images, and the like—is essential to helping us remember and process information. If you want a goal indelibly seared into your brain, so vibrantly alive in the forefront of your mind that you can't possibly push it aside or forget about it, you need to animate it. Wherever possible, take advantage of the power of pictures.

By the way, it's not an either/or situation. We're not all of a sudden going to drop using words and numbers and start drawing stick figures (abandoning language and reverting to cave drawings is not exactly an evolutionary step forward). Words and pictures aren't enemies of one another. Rather, they are great friends that work together to give our thoughts and experiences, and especially our goals, deeper meaning. Together they help us believe in our goals and charge us to take action. "Visual processing is the primary sense our brain uses to interpret the meaning of language," says Nanci Bell, one of the top minds in language expression and comprehension. "Our visual sense, in the formal of visual imagery, integrates with language more easily and efficiently than the other four senses."[4]

Sometimes it's not possible to show an actual visual. Going back to our earlier example where we were trying to convince the world of the colorlessness problem, you might not always be able to channel your inner Ross Perot and whip out some poster board charts. If you're giving a speech to thousands of employees on the factory floor, or standing and holding a drink at a cocktail party, drawing a picture might be awkward. But you can certainly use your words to control the imagery and generate a great mental visual.

Great politicians are masters of speaking visually. In 1961, President Kennedy gave a speech to a joint session of Congress to discuss his plans for putting a man on the moon. You're doubtless familiar with the line, "I believe that this nation should commit itself to achieving the goal, before this decade is out, of landing a man on the moon and returning him safely to the earth."

When Martin Luther King Jr. stood on the steps of the Lincoln Memorial, he said, "I have a dream that one day on the red hills of Georgia, the sons of former slaves and the sons of former slave owners will be able to sit down together at the table of brotherhood."

The narration for Ronald Reagan's famous 1984 reelection ad began, "It's morning again in America. Today more men and women will go to work than ever before in our country's history. With interest rates at about half the record highs of 1980, nearly 2,000 families today will buy new homes, more than at any time in the past four years. This afternoon 6,500 young men and women will be married, and with inflation at less than half of what it was just four years ago, they can look forward with confidence to the future."

In each of these examples, you can literally picture the words being spoken in your mind, create an animated version of what is being said. Can you picture the man on the moon? Can you visualize a former slave and a former slave owner sitting together? If you close your eyes, can you imagine what a beautiful morning in America looks like? You and millions of others could see those pictures, and it's one of the reasons these great leaders occupy the place they do in our history.

## MAKE YOUR GOALS VISUAL

Brian Scudamore is a high school dropout who talked his way into college. If you've ever gone through the college application process for yourself or your kids, you know that's an impressive feat all on its own. But what about the fact that, once enrolled, he then checked himself out of his higher education a year before graduation in order to create an empire from a pile of trash?

Scudamore started 1-800-Got-Junk (which, as the company name implies, specializes in junk removal) in 1989 with just $700 and a beat-up old pickup truck. In the first five years he grew revenues from $201,532 to $8,057,563. The secret behind his overwhelming success? "Have a clear vision," Scudamore says. "Know what your future looks like, feels like, and acts like. . . . Latch onto that picture as though it has already happened. . . . [Then] share it with your team so they can see it and do what it takes to achieve it."[5] In other words, draw a picture of your goal.

One way Scudamore brings his visions to life is through the use of a "Vision Wall," a space that claims some major wall real estate at 1-800-Got-Junk's home office, or the Junktion, as it's called. "If you can't see your vision come true, you'll never have enough faith in it to achieve it," Scudamore told *Profit* magazine in 2008. Company aspirations posted on the 1-800-Got-Junk's Vision Wall have included a goal for the company to appear on "Oprah"—something many small business owners dream of, but which Scudamore actually made happen.

And it's not just the CEO's ideas that are posted under the sign that reads, "Can You Imagine?" Employees are encouraged to submit their visions as well. Marketing manager Andrea Baxter had to campaign to get her idea of "Can you imagine our brand appearing on Starbucks cups everywhere?" on the wall. It seemed an impossible quest, a HARD Goal that even Scudamore thought was too difficult to achieve. But Baxter persisted that she saw it happening, and so up on the wall it went.

As a result (and with a lot of elbow grease on Baxter's part), the quote on No. 70 in Starbucks' "The Way I See It" series cups belongs to Scudamore and 1-800-Got-Junk. It reads, "It's difficult for people to get rid of junk. They get attached to things and let them define who they are. If there's one thing I've learned in this business, it's that you are what you can't let go of." Baxter couldn't let go of her vision. It became an integral part of her being, and so she was able to successfully rethink what was possible. By the way, the whole cup thing translated into about 10 million cups that came into the hands of Starbucks customers all across North America. Not too shabby a vision to attain.

So, how do you animate your HARD Goals? The answer is, start simply, with a picture. I don't care if you can't draw (I certainly can't). Together we're going to create a fully animated vision of your goal that lives in your mind. A vision that's so crystal clear you'll swear you already achieved your goal.

Here's how it works: If your goal is to lose weight, envision how your body will look, feel, and move at your goal weight. For instance, what will it be like to close the button on your jeans and still have room in your waistband to spare? Do you envision a silent moment of pride, or do you see yourself running out into the living room to exuberantly show anyone who is home? If your goal is to quit smoking, you might visualize yourself energetically playing with your kids. Maybe you're mountain biking as a family in the Rockies or even riding the waves in Malibu. You're all together, laughing, wet, a bit chilly but who cares, and best of all, you can breathe and keep up just fine. Or your animated goal might be more solitary: just you, sitting in the morning sun enjoying a cup of coffee without a cigarette. How incredible does that vision make you feel?

You might create a clear mental picture of yourself secretly jumping for joy like a lunatic in the stairwell at work after receiving that promotion you're after. What about hugging your friends as you cross the marathon finish line? Can you feel that hard-earned sweat pouring down your back? How about visualizing the post-race carb-loaded meal you can't wait to order from your favorite restaurant and chow down on? Or perhaps your goal is retirement in Boca. Can you feel the green grass beneath your feet and take in the amazing smell coming from that gardenia bush over there? How does it make you feel on an emotional level to realize that, from here on in, your time is 100 percent yours?

Whatever you intend to achieve with your goal, animate it, right down to the minute details. If your goal is to double your company's market share, maybe you'll picture . . . Well, huh, that's a tough one. And here you can start to see a problem with a lot of goals. Too many goals, especially those in the corporate or financial realms, are too abstract to turn into a picture. And that's a major problem, given that I've just spent several pages showing you all this great research about how we need to visualize.

## THE NEED FOR SPECIFICITY

In the business world especially, much gets made of the need to have highly specific goals, and I couldn't agree more. The problem is that when a lot of people talk about specificity, what they really mean is that the goal needs to be described as a number. And I'm sorry to say that if you don't first start with a picture, those numbers will provide a very false sense of specificity.

In the early 1990s, Sears assigned its auto repair staff a revenue quota of $147 per hour. Pretty specific, right? Well it turns out it wasn't specific enough because staff members started overcharging for work and doing unnecessary repairs. Then-chairman Edward Brennan acknowledged that Sears' "goal setting process for service advisers created an environment where mistakes did occur."[6]

American Airlines has had a reputation for specific goals, right down to the departmental—and even the individual—level. If a plane is late, American wants to know whose fault it is. So when a plane is late, what's the employees' reaction? They make sure they don't get blamed for failing to hit their goal. Oh sure, the plane may sit on the tarmac for a while, making your life miserable as a passenger, but that gate agent hit his or her specific goal. Woo-hoo! By contrast, an airline like Southwest Airlines thinks about a "team delay." They don't care too much about attributing a delay to an individual; instead they care about getting the plane in the air for the customers and then figuring out how to prevent delays in the future.

If somebody picks a number without first creating a picture, it's a cop-out. It's not specific. Being specific is when you can tell me every little nuance of what that number translates into out in the real world. I can pick numbers out of thin air all day long, but they don't tell me a darn thing unless I know what they mean. Think about it. Which airline truly has more specific goals? The one with numbers assigned to every individual? Or the one with fewer numbers but a very clear picture of what the customer should be experiencing?

I call this the "illusion of specificity." It's when we've got numbers assigned to our goals, but we don't know what the heck they mean. Sounds good, looks good, but it doesn't mean squat. Sears' employees had a specific number, but they didn't have a specific understanding of what that number really meant. Remember in the last chapter when I told you how GM executives wore buttons bearing the numeral "29" as a constant reminder of the company's lofty goal of 29 percent U.S. market share? And then I noted that nobody's going to develop a deep emotional attachment to a number? Well, not only is this true, but there's another problem as well: it's very difficult to develop a memorable picture around an abstract number such as a market share figure. And if you can't develop a memorable picture, you won't really have a memorable goal—and a goal that you can't remember will never get accomplished.

Numerical success (such as doubling market share) is epiphenomenal. What's that mean? It means it's "the result of" something else. Had GM hit its 29 percent market share, it would have been "the result of" something else, like having cars that people wanted to buy, made without any defects, by engaged and productive employees, and sold through dealers that had killer salespeople and high-touch customer service. And, not coincidentally, I could create very concrete pictures for any of those other factors much more easily than I could for the 29 percent market share. Seriously, if I gave you a crayon and paper, which is easier to draw—high-touch customer service, cutting-edge car design and excited customers, or 29 percent market share? Here's my real test of specificity: my kids could draw pictures of everything except the 29 percent. If a six-year-old can draw a picture of your goal, it's specific. If not, it needs more work.

Now let's be clear; I'm not saying you don't need numbers. On the contrary, great companies like Apple, Google, and Starbucks all use numbers. But they get millions of people aligned, excited, passionate, and devoted because they've drawn a picture underlying those numbers that's immediately accessible to the mind of every employee, customer, and investor. Numbers are nice and easy measuring sticks to see how much progress you've made toward achieving the goal in your picture. But they're means to an end, not the end itself. It's the goal in your picture that really represents your end.

What's the goal of Apple's iPod? As Steve Jobs said when it launched, it's like having "1,000 songs in your pocket." You'll notice that Apple used a number, but it was a concrete number. (I can easily picture 1,000 songs, on CDs, floating in air and then shrinking into my iPod, can't you?) And then, of course, there's the MacBook Air, otherwise known as "The world's thinnest notebook." Sounds slim, but still a pretty solid concept to me. Ba-dumm-bumm.

Likewise when Google founders Sergey Brin and Larry Page walked into venture capital firm Sequoia Capital to get funding for their start-up search engine company. They said the goal of Google was to "provide access to the world's information in one click."[7] Or consider how Starbucks founder Howard Schultz described the goal of his company: "Starbucks creates a third place between work and home." In the best companies, you'll find that their goals sound a lot like their marketing, which sounds a lot like their vision. Employees, customers, investors, and the press can all vividly picture the company's goals. In a phrase, they have "message consistency."

In each one of the above examples I can concretely picture the proposed goal. I can see (and hear) someone clicking a mouse for Google. I can imagine what that "third place" looks like for Starbucks right down to the pervading coffee-bean smell and how happy people's faces will look once they realize they have such a place. And I can certainly picture the world's thinnest notebook right down to what it would be like to hold it in my hands.

Take 1-800-Got-Junk's vision board. In addition to sales goals, Scudamore and his staff embraced mental pictures of goals like getting on "Oprah," an organizational chart listing positions that didn't even exist yet, or a map of all the cities they'd be in that they hadn't yet penetrated. They saw it all as clearly as if it had already happened and then worked toward making those visions a reality. These kinds of HARD Goals are rarely accomplished with abstract ideas. However, goose those goals up with some animated thinking, and you're well on your way. I might not know what $100 million looks like, but I can picture what it feels like to walk on stage after being introduced by Oprah. I can also hear the roar of the crowd (OK, I'm a big dreamer) and imagine how excited and nervous I would be. Just as I can envision an expanded organizational chart and having a franchise in Pittsburgh. And if I can picture it, it's that much easier for me to build some excitement around achieving it.

What about those companies that are absolutely wedded to their goal-setting worksheets and online forms that only offer a place for a single number to describe their goal? One of our clients, a North American division of a European company, had a software application for recording its goals that only gave people a small blank for inputting a number. The parent company's leaders didn't want vividly written descriptions, they wanted a GM-style number. (I think they were really hoping for everyone to write "29 percent.")

So given everything we've just learned, what did this division do? Well, the leaders weren't big fans of committing career suicide, so they turned themselves into a test case. First, they completed the online forms with a number, as the software required. But then everybody, including the CEO, scanned their hand-drawn goal pictures, and with the OK from corporate, they attached those scanned picture files to their goals in the software system. And then, of course, they taped those pictures to their office or cubicle walls and did everything we've been talking about in this chapter. By the way, they'll be moving to using "animated" goals for a few more regions this year. Why? This is the only division worldwide where over 90 percent of managers hit their stretch goals. (All the other divisions are below 30 percent.)

Of course, everything I just said about business goals applies to other goals like personal health, savings, or retirement goals. Any goal, be it personal or professional, that stays strictly in the abstract will never deliver the same kind of outcome and process stimulation as will goals that are animated.

"Two years ago I never dreamed I'd be setting weekly speed and distance goals for my swimming," says Ivy Lynn, a retired elementary school teacher in her early 50s. "Back then I was recovering from a hip replacement operation and pretty consumed with wondering if I would ever walk normally again." Swimming, a sport Ivy had never even considered previously, was part of her rehabilitation process. "I fell in love with being in the water," Ivy says, brushing her blond curls out of the way to reveal eyes that burn bright with excitement. "Something suddenly happened where I stopped seeing myself as an invalid and started picturing myself, yes, 51-year-old me, swimming laps. I could barely make it up my front steps at the time, but I saw myself quite clearly as a swimmer."

"Suddenly I was telling people, 'I'm going to be a competitive swimmer,' and everyone was looking at me hobbling around on my walker like I was nuts. Even my husband was rolling his eyes at me." Ivy set her goal into motion by creating a collage of inspiring images, her own version of a vision board. "I cut out a bunch of pictures of water, people swimming, famous swimmers, and plastered them all over a piece of poster board. It was the kind of thing I would have had my kids do back when I was teaching. It probably sounds crazy, but I could see myself in every one of those pictures right down to my killer swimmer's bod, which I definitely did not have at the time."

Ivy competed in her first meet last month. She came in fourth. "I'm not saying it's the Olympics, but that was never my goal. I just wanted to be the best swimmer I could be, and that's exactly what I see myself working toward every day," she says. It's been a while since Ivy made a vision board; she's been too busy training with her coach. But the other day she stopped by the crafts store to buy a piece of poster board. "I have a plan," Ivy says, "a new goal, really. I want to swim in waters all over the world. Like the Dead Sea and the Arabian Ocean, which I hear in some places is the most gorgeous color of emerald green. So I'm putting together some images to help inspire me to make it happen. I told my husband last night that he should start thinking about packing for Yemen around July. He thinks I'm kidding, but honestly, I'll be pretty surprised if it doesn't happen. I can already see myself there."

## RULES FOR MAKING A PICTURE

Just like Ivy, when you begin to create an animated goal in your head, you don't need to use words. You'll add them in a bit, but at first, start by thinking solely about the graphic representation of your goal. Once you get that picture, start to add some detail to really make it vivid in your mind.

I created the following nine dimensions to help you really bring your animated goal to life by focusing on different aspects of the visual representation or image of your goal. (I don't expect to turn everyone into an artist, but these questions are not dissimilar to what an art teacher might ask a student.) We'll start with the most concrete and then move into the finer details.

- **Size:** How big is your picture or the things you see in your visualization of your goal? Are you living in a small or big beach house? Is your "better than the iPad" invention bigger than the Kindle? Is your cutting-edge electric car the size of a Lumina or an Escalade? How many square feet is your "third place" coffee shop? Is it bigger or smaller than your kitchen at home?

- **Color:** What colors do you see? Color is especially important in stirring up meaning and emotion for your goals. It affects us each individually on a very deep unconscious level. Even a single color can radically affect our moods, perceptions, and thoughts. So look closely at the picture of your goal so you see everything that's there. For instance, is your skin tanned after losing all that weight, since you're now spending so much time in a bathing suit out by the pool? Or just how blue is the ocean outside your new beach house? You might even decide to emphasize certain features of your goal with special colors to create greater excitement. Or downplay some aspects of your goal that might otherwise deter you by setting them in black and white. If strawberry cheesecake is your diet weakness, seeing yourself turning it down in black and white may make it easier (and a lot less appetizing) than having to face all that creamy yellow and sticky red decadence.

• **Shape:** What shapes are visible? Shape also influences us to feel emotions. In fact, scientists have been studying the effects of "angry" triangles and "loving" circles since the 1940s. Is your belly rounder or more angular after dropping those 30 pounds? I don't know about you, but the image of a flat stomach certainly puts an extra spring in my step and helps me to keep saying no to "forbidden" foods. Henry Moore, the famous sculptor, is quoted as saying, "Our knowledge of shape and form remains, in general, a mixture of visual and tactile experiences. . . . A child learns about roundness from handling a ball far more than from looking at it." So don't just see the shapes in your goals, feel them. Are they smooth or rough, heavy or light? If your goal is to get more organized, what does it feel like to run your hand along the smooth flat plane of your desk with no clutter to block the motion?

• **Distinct parts:** How many different and distinct parts make up the whole of your goal, and how do those parts fit together or work in tandem to create the outcome you desire? Say your goal is to get a raise at work. First, you might have to make some changes in your work ethic, maybe put in some extra hours or weekends or take on a special project. Perhaps from there your sales will increase or you'll have succeeded in overhauling a struggling department. Then there will be the inevitable meeting with the boss to discuss your accomplishments and what you think is a suitable reward. Finally, there will be the day your increased paycheck arrives and how you'll celebrate your accomplishment. What will that extra money mean to your life, to your family? Will it allow you to move into a bigger house or take more frequent vacations? Maybe you plan to funnel it all into a college fund for your kids and you won't even really feel the impact of it for another 15 years. And finally, how does it make you feel about yourself to have accomplished this HARD Goal?

- **Setting:** Where is this picture taking place? Just like in a great novel, the setting of your goal will influence its outcome. I'm talking about more than just a room or a place. Season, time, objects, weather, and so much more can be part of the setting for your goal. A lot of successful diet goals have been built around the looming vision of bathing suit season. Where does your goal take place, what does it look like and smell like? Does it feel relaxed, celebratory, or even a little bit scary or sad? Sometimes achieving our goals means giving up things from our past that, while we accept, we never quite overcome. As a former smoker, I admit, I'll always miss just a little bit the rush of sucking nicotine into my body. And even though my thoughts, feelings, and moods are a lot happier without this toxin, there are moments when I grieve its loss. It's not a bad thing, it's just reality.

- **Background:** What's going on in the background? Parenthetically, sometimes in pictures like this, other unconscious goals start to creep into your background, making them feel pretty important, thus increasing your eagerness to attain them. "Sure, I want to double sales; but why do I need a cheering audience when I announce our sales figures? Oh, right, because one of my unspoken goals is my deep-seated desire to be adored."

- **Lighting:** Describe the lighting. If you've ever had the winter blues, you know how important lighting can be in determining your mood and energy level. That's not to say all your goals have to take place in well-lit rooms or the sun in order to be effective. What you envision may only be possible at night or in the rain or snow. If your goal is to night ski at Chamonix, you're wasting your time if you envision yourself riding the lift at daybreak.

• **Emotions:** What are you feeling? And if there are other people in the picture, what are they feeling? And how do you know? What facial expressions, body language, or other indications do you see? When Mary, a breast cancer survivor, saw herself once again well and running in her first Race for the Cure, she pictured her husband and daughter cheering her on from the sidelines. She could also imagine exactly how amazing it would feel at that moment when she crossed the finish line. But she also focused on how it would feel knowing she had helped raise money for other women like her, and that maybe her efforts would make a difference in someone else's life.

• **Movement:** Are you or any other people doing things? Not a tough question if yours is an action goal like learning to ski or to master French cooking. But what about more sedentary goals? What kind of movement will you find in a goal to be smarter with your money, get more sleep, or have more patience? It's there, you just may have to look a little harder to see it.

I'm not asking you to think about all these various aspects because I want you to get hung up on great art. Rather, I'm doing it to maximize your neuroanatomy: your nervous system. We humans are evolutionarily wired for visual, not textual, stimuli. We're only in existence today because we got sufficiently adept at visually recognizing dangers like saber-toothed tigers hiding on top of rocks or in the grass—and then using those same visual abilities to invent protection in the way of spears, arrows, and the like.

Brent Hardgrave is one of the top hairstylists in the world. He's the first American stylist ever given the honor of International Artisan by Keune Haircosmetics. And without knowing it, you've probably seen his work everywhere from celebrity weddings to the pages of *Esquire*.

Brent innovated a particular dry haircutting technique. At the risk of stereotyping, the women reading this will probably know what I'm talking about better than the guys. So, fellas, let me put it like this: One of the perks of writing books is getting the occasional test-drive. Brent cut my hair using this technique, and when I got home, my wife took one look at me, and, well, let's just say it's good the kids weren't home. Then my wife had Brent cut her hair, and she was so ecstatic about it that when she got home, well, Brent's my new best friend.

So, back to the cool haircutting technique. Brent told me, "I could picture the cut perfectly. I knew how I would hold the scissors, how I would shape the hair, what each strand of hair would do." Brent had his new technique pictured so clearly in his mind that he realized he faced a huge roadblock: normal scissors just don't do what he needed them to do. It's at this point that a lot of putative innovators (whether people or companies) turn back; lots of people are addicted to the word *can't*. But not innovators like Steve Jobs, Jeff Bezos, or in this case, Brent.

Armed with the perfect picture of what he needed (first mental, then physical), Brent designed just the right scissor for this cut and then called a scissor manufacturer. It turned out that the manufacturer he called had been prototyping a similar scissor, but it wasn't quite "there" yet. So they put their visions together, and thus was born a new kind of curved scissor. It's due out soon (as of the writing of this book), and it's already generating lots of buzz in their industry. Brent's perfect mental picture is about to be a reality for his clients (which, for obvious reasons, now include my wife and me).

Molecular biologist John Medina tells us that right now our color vision and sense of smell are fighting for "evolutionary control" (to be the first sense involved when something in the outside world happens).[8] Furthermore, our vision is winning; "about 60% of our smell-related genes have been permanently damaged in this neural arbitrage, and they are marching towards obsolescence at a rate fourfold faster than any other species sampled." Why? Because the visual and olfactory cortexes take up a lot of space, and something has to give.

If even drawing a stick causes you to break into a cold sweat, you might want to consider constructing what's often known as a vision wall (in corporate settings) or vision board (for individuals). A vision wall or board is basically a way of creating a picture for people who are terrified of drawing (or who have a hyper-specific goal like getting on "Oprah"). Instead of whipping out the markers, you take a wall or piece of paper and start pasting pictures, visuals, sticky notes, or anything else that will help you visualize your goal. If you've ever flipped through a magazine and felt yourself drawn to a color, a texture, or a picture of something you've never before seen, you've experienced the pull of the subconscious. Your vision board doesn't have to make clear sense to anyone but you. In other words, there's no real wrong or right. It's your goal, and you're allowed to see it however you like.

So if you've got an artistic bent, go ahead and start to sketch or paint; otherwise, break out the old magazines and get scissor and glue crazy. Don't think too much about what you are trying to create, go more with your gut than your head. You can always remake and refine your board when the vision of your goal becomes clearer. For right now, you're just trying to get at the pulse of it all—the basic colors, shapes, sizes, and emotions.

## WHOSE PERSPECTIVE?

I really want you to give those visual skills a workout—again, not to develop your artistic talent, but rather to sear the picture of your goal into your memory. The artists out there will notice that I didn't mention perspective. That's because perspective deserves a special mention. Imagine you've just created a highly detailed picture of yourself having achieved your weight-loss goals (nice body, by the way). Now the question becomes, how do you see yourself? Are you looking at the picture of yourself from outside of yourself (like a spouse, friend, or even stranger looking at you)? Or are you looking through your own eyes (like you're looking at yourself in the mirror)? Seems like a semantic difference, doesn't it? Turns out the difference is way bigger than you'd think.

Some Oxford University researchers gave subjects 100 different positive messages (like "It's Saturday morning—the start of the weekend . . .") and asked them to do a little visualization exercise, imagining themselves in a particular situation. The subjects were divided up, and two of the groups were assigned to imagine themselves either from a first-person perspective (looking through their own eyes) or a third-person perspective (looking at themselves as though through someone else's eyes).

The people who imagined themselves looking through their own eyes reported significantly higher positive reactions than those who viewed themselves through a third-person perspective.

Of course, this works in the other direction as well. Patients with PTSD (post-traumatic stress disorder) report less anxiety when they recall traumatic events from the third-person perspective. Evidently, the third-person perspective is useful for taking scary or traumatic images and making them less scary or traumatic by sucking out all of their emotional power. Of course, that is a double-edged sword because in studies of depressed people, when they recall autobiographical memories, there's a lot more third-person perspective going on than with people who've never been depressed. This implies that depressed people are unknowingly using the power of the third-person perspective in a bad way, because they're sucking all the joyful emotions out of their mental pictures.

When creating a mental picture of your goals, it's important to use a first-person perspective. After all, this is your story, your goal, and no one but you is qualified to animate it. If you're looking at your newly svelte body, do it as though you're looking at yourself in the mirror and not the way your spouse or partner or friends will see you. If you've just unveiled your super-amazing new product, make sure you see yourself standing at the podium looking at the audience or looking at the device you hold in your own hands. You'll get a lot more mental bang for your visualization buck if your animated goal is 100 percent from your point of view.

## WRITE IT DOWN

Once you've got a picture of your goal clearly set in your mind, it's time to write it all down. You've no doubt heard for years that writing things down helps you remember them better. However, if, like most folks, you've never been told why it's so important to write things down, your attitude is probably something along the lines of "why bother." And who can blame you? It's a lot of extra work to write something down when you can just as easily store it in your brain. Isn't it?

The answer to that is no. Writing things down works on two levels: external storage and encoding. External storage is easy to explain: you're storing the information contained in your goal in a location (such as a piece of paper) that is very easy to access and review at any time. You could post that paper in your office, on your refrigerator, or elsewhere. It doesn't take a neuroscientist to know you will remember something much better if you're staring at a visual cue that serves as a reminder every single day.

But there's another deeper phenomenon happening: encoding. Encoding is the biological process by which the things we perceive travel to our brain's hippocampus, where they're analyzed. From there decisions are made about what gets stored in our long-term memory and, in turn, what gets discarded. Writing improves that encoding process. In other words, when you write something down it has a much greater chance of being remembered.

Neuropsychologists have identified the "generation effect," which basically says individuals demonstrate better memory for material they've generated themselves than for material they've merely read. It's a nice edge to have, and when you write down your picture, you get to access the generation effect twice: first, when you generate the goal and create a picture in your mind, and second, when you write it down, because you're essentially reprocessing or regenerating that image. You have to rethink your mental picture, put it on the paper, place objects, scale them, think about their spatial relations, draw facial expressions, and so on. There's a lot of cognitive processing taking place right there. In essence, you get a double whammy that really sears the goal into your brain.

Study after study shows you will remember things better when you write them down. Typically, subjects for these types of studies are students taking notes in class. However, one group of researchers looked at people conducting hiring interviews. When the interviewers took notes about their interviews with each of the candidates, they were able to recall about 23 percent more nuggets of information from the interviews than people who didn't take notes. Parenthetically, if you're being interviewed for a job and you want the interviewer to remember you, you'd better hope he or she is taking notes.

It's not just general recall that improves when you write things down. Doing so will also improve your recall of the really important information. You know how when you're in a classroom setting there's some stuff the teacher says that's really important (it'll be on the test), and then there's the not so important (it won't be on the test)? Well, one study found that when people weren't taking notes in class, they remembered just as many unimportant facts as they did important facts. (There's a recipe for a C grade.) But when people were taking notes, they remembered many more important facts and many fewer unimportant facts (and that, my friends, is the secret of A students). Writing things down doesn't just help you remember, it makes your mind more efficient by helping you focus on the truly important stuff. And your HARD Goals absolutely qualify as truly important stuff.

Geena is a radiologist at a busy city hospital. She also has a physician husband whose social job demands keep her running and three kids with equally busy schedules to take care of. "Trying to accomplish anything for myself is almost impossible," Geena says with a good-natured smile. "But I've been running marathons since college, and it's one thing I demand remains mine."

Geena has to play a bit of a trick on her brain in order to find the time to train and run. "If I tell myself it's all about me, I start to feel guilty. Instead of running I could be helping my husband or going to one of my kids' games or events." So Geena only signs herself up for charity runs, "Not exactly a difficult endeavor in this day and age when we are running to raise money for everything from cancer to animal rights," Geena remarks.

"It's easy to see myself running, I love it," she says. "But the part that's really essential for me to get down on paper, and to review every day so I stick to my goal, is how my running will bring benefit to really worthy causes. I mean, I really try to see the faces of the people I am going to help. Otherwise I'll cave and stay home and bake cookies for my kids instead of finding the time to fit in my four miles."

Geena has a heartfelt connection to her goal to run. But without the aid of a clear vision, and the written version of that vision to keep her on track, she's the first to admit she probably wouldn't see it through.

## DRAW WITH YOUR WORDS

Remember at the beginning of the chapter when I said that great goal setters, like Kennedy, King, and Reagan, were masters of using highly visual language? Well, I want to give you one more technique so that should you find yourself in a situation that doesn't allow for pictures, you can draw with your words.

To begin, whenever you talk about a goal, you want to use really concrete words. Allan Paivio, now professor emeritus at the University of Western Ontario, is the scientist who pioneered the concept of concrete words. In one of my favorite studies, Paivio analyzed people's ability to remember concrete words as compared to abstract words.[9] Concrete words have high "imagery value," that is, you can picture what they refer to. For example, words like *road*, *bridge*, *clown*, and even *picture* are all pretty concrete. But words like *condition*, *amount*, *request*, and *purpose* are all pretty abstract. Paivio paired concrete nouns and adjectives and tested them against paired abstract nouns and adjectives to see which words were easier to recall. Some of the word pairs were related, like *young lady*, and some were not, like *soft lady*.

In every case, recall was better for concrete word pairs than it was for abstract word pairs. It's just easier to remember *dead body* or *happy clown* than it is *essential nutrient* or *significant result*. In fact, and this is critical, you'll remember totally unrelated concrete word pairs way better than you'll remember related abstract word pairs. Across Paivio's experiments, concrete word pairs could be remembered as much as two to three times more frequently than the abstract word pairs.

Now here's the real kicker: almost anyone who's ever set a goal for someone else, for instance a corporate CEO, suffers from abstract word disease. Let me share some of the actual abstract word pairs tested in Paivio's study:

Complete set
Annual event
Useful purpose
Original finding
Critical condition

Reasonable request
Constant attention
Adequate amount
Significant result
Possible guess

If you've ever read a corporate goal-setting memo, I guarantee you've seen word pairs like this, if not these exact ones. Over and over again people set goals using abstract language. Then they look around bewildered as to why nobody remembers what they said. But the reason is that they are using language that is guaranteed not to be remembered.

I've had the word choice conversation with a lot of CEOs. And while hundreds of them have gotten it, no problem, there are thousands more that failed to achieve "significant results" on their goal-setting memos because they obtusely refused to give "constant attention" to this issue. See how easy it is to slip into that crappy abstract language without even noticing? It's a disease. If you want goals that people (including yourself) will drip blood, sweat, and tears to achieve, you had better address your abstract word disease, and fast.

So the next time you're about to give a speech or have a conversation about goals, ask yourself this question: Could the people listening to me draw a picture of what I'm saying? Or even better, "Could a six-year-old draw a picture of what I'm saying?" Back to those earlier world-leader examples: my kids could easily draw a man on the moon, a former slave and a former slave owner sitting together, and a beautiful morning in America. Can the same be said of your goals?

Why are concrete words so much better, the scientific types out there are no doubt asking. Paivio's argument (formally known as dual-coding theory) is that concrete words get access to a right-hemisphere, image-based system in addition to a verbal system. A competing argument says that concrete words activate a broader contextual verbal support but do not access a distinct image-based system. Who's right? Well, some recent fMRI studies detected the brain regions involved in encoding concrete versus abstract nouns and found that, here's a shock, there's probably a good bit of truth in both theories.

## A LOT OF GENIUSES ARE VISUAL

If you embrace the science of thinking visually, you're not alone. You're joining some of the greatest minds in history. "Tesla came to the idea of the self-starting motor one evening as he was reciting a poem by Goethe and watching a sunset. Suddenly he imagined a magnetic field rapidly rotating inside a circle of electromagnets. The energized-circle imagery apparently was suggested by the disk of the sun and the pulse of rotation by the poem's rhythm." So writes John Briggs regarding the great physicist and inventor Nikola Tesla in his wonderful book on the process of creative genius.

Tesla devoted his lifetime to rethinking the possible. And we know from his own recorded words the substantial role animated visualization played in his many successes. "Before I put a sketch on paper, the whole idea is worked out mentally. In my mind I change the construction, make improvements, and even operate the device. Without ever having drawn a sketch I can give the measurements of all parts to workmen, and when completed all these parts will fit, just as certainly as though I had made the actual drawings."[10]

Thanks to Telsa's animated thinking, we have AC current, the hydroelectric dam, and the radio, to name just a very few of his more than 100 patented and countless unpatented inventions. I read recently that, in 1909, Tesla told *Popular Mechanics*, "It will soon be possible to transmit wireless messages all over the world so simply that any individual can carry and operate his own apparatus." The apparatus, Tesla predicted, would be about the size of a pocket watch. Tesla's vision might sound a lot like an iPhone or BlackBerry, and he came up with it at a time when the rotary phone (for those who remember such) was still decades in the making.

Tesla is far from one of a kind. Many of the greatest minds throughout history have visualized, imagined, envisioned, or, to use the word that titles this chapter, animated their ideas and goals. For instance, sculptor Henry Moore, who, Briggs tells us, imagined his sculptures, no matter their size, as though he were holding them in the palm of his hand. Briggs relays how Moore mentally visualized a complex form, knowing what all sides looked like, even realizing the sculpture's volume by knowing the space that the shape displaced in the air. Or the great anthropologist Claude Lévi-Strauss, another of Briggs's studies, who saw three-dimensional schematic pictures in his mind when working through ethnographic problems.

The great physicist and Nobel laureate Richard Feynman described his use of "visual animation" in his memoirs as follows:[11]

I had a scheme, which I still use today, when somebody is explaining something that I'm trying to understand: I keep making up examples. For instance, the mathematicians would come in with a terrific theorem, and they're all excited. As they're telling me the conditions of the theorem, I construct something in my mind which fits all the conditions. You know, you have a set (one ball), disjoint (two balls). Then the balls turn colors, grow hairs, or whatever, in my head as they put more conditions on. Finally they state the theorem, which is some dumb thing about the ball which isn't true for my hairy green ball thing, so I say "False!" . . . I guessed right most of the time.

Michelangelo, Amelia Earhart, Mozart, Albert Einstein, Georgia O'Keeffe, Muhammad Ali, Mia Hamm, Ansel Adams, Michael Jordan, and Bruce Lee (I think there's someone in there for everyone), and so many more respected names, all share a common link. They all used or use the process of animation to unleash their creative genius, to reach their goals, and to achieve amazing results.

Undeniably, injecting life into our thoughts and goals is correlated with genius. And who of us couldn't use a dash or two of genius when it comes to our HARD Goals? Never again will you stare blankly at a computer screen that says, "The Company will double market share in a year" or a sticky note on your bathroom mirror that says, "I will lose 30 pounds in six months." Your goals, once properly animated, will vividly play before your eyes as did Feynman's mental cartoons or Moore's three-dimensional miniature sculptures or Tesla's synesthetic visions. And, just like these great creative minds, through animating your goals, you will get the burst of drive you need to take your HARD Goals from vision to reality.

## SUMMARY

The biggest impediment to any goal is lack of visual stimulation. We're human, and so we're visual, and our brains remember pictures better than they do words. So why not make it work for you and not against you? Start with a first-person perspective and draw a picture or make a collage or vision board of your goal that captures specific elements like size, color, shape, distinct parts, setting, background, lighting, emotions, and movement. Then write your goal down using concrete words that will sear it into your brain.

I'm not saying every one of your HARD Goals will make you an Einstein. But if you follow the rules in this chapter, you'll certainly be acting like him. After all, this is the guy who, while describing how he used visual imagery to think, said, "I very rarely think in words at all."

The story goes that one day Albert took a nap on a sunny hillside. The sun's rays filtered through his half-closed eyelids, and he imagined himself sitting on one of the sun's rays, traveling deep into the universe. At the end of his journey he found himself right back where he started, napping on that hillside. This visualization allowed him to see the "space-time" curve, and so was born the general theory of relativity, a radical departure from the popular physics and mathematical thinking of the day. That's a pretty big push for the power of visualization (and napping).

Get more examples and tools at hardgoals.com.

# 3

# Required

"I'll start tomorrow." Three words that are the death knell for goals. Because how many times have you said "tomorrow" when what you really meant was "never"? I know, as the words tumble from your mouth you believe them: "I'll start a diet tomorrow." You feel strong, resolved, and 100 percent committed to your goal. It seems as if nothing can come between you and the promise of tomorrow. A tomorrow that really will be the first day of the rest of your life.

But then tomorrow actually comes. And once again, we face that same decision: start right now or postpone starting for one more day. C'mon, it's just one day, right? Seriously, how bad is it really going to be to postpone for one more day? The answer, of course, is that postponing for one day probably isn't the worst thing ever—except that one day is never one day.

One day becomes two, two days become three, and three days become years.

Putting off until tomorrow what you should be doing today is a problem that keeps a lot of people from achieving their goals. Three-quarters of college students consider themselves procrastinators,[1] and some estimates figure that 20 percent of the adult population could be classified as "chronic procrastinators."[2] But as bad as these figures are, they understate the problem when it comes to HARD Goals. For instance, in one of our recent studies, 77 percent of people admitted to having put off starting a diet. And, compared to non-procrastinators (you know, the people who actually started their diets), the folks who postponed their diets were eight times more likely to be unhappy with their current weight.

Piers Steel at the University of Calgary, one of the great procrastination researchers, in reviewing hundreds of studies, overwhelmingly found that putting things off doesn't create happiness.[3] In fact, a whopping 94 percent of people said procrastination hurt their happiness. Additionally, employees who procrastinate keep worrying about work long after they've left the office, and student procrastination is firmly related to lower course grades, lower overall grades, and lower exam scores. Procrastination is also strongly linked to poor health (that's what happens when you put off necessary medical tests) and powerfully correlated to poorer financial health.

Procrastination can also pose another financial risk. Every person in America intellectually knows that getting your taxes done early can help you avoid errors made when rushing. And yet, a 2002 survey by H&R Block found that waiting until the last minute on taxes cost the average person $400 because the process was rushed and mistakes were made. The net effect was $473 million in overpayments across the country.

Amazingly, it's not just difficult goals that we put off; we also procrastinate on fun and entertaining stuff. The financial researchers in TowerGroup report that each year Americans spend about $65 billion on gift cards, and recipients fail to redeem $6.8 billion of them. Not that it's all bad for the companies that issue them: in 2009, Home Depot Inc. reported $37 million in revenue from unused gift card credit.

I don't share all these negative studies and statistics just to bring you down. Rather, the information is intended as a learning tool to help you recognize and overcome your own issues with procrastination. Look, if you really want to achieve something, if you have a heartfelt connection to losing 20 pounds, starting a business, becoming fluent in Italian, or whatever your goal is, you absolutely can do it. You just need to rally your inner strength so you actually start and stick to that goal. And the most efficient way to do that is to infuse your goal with a feeling of urgency—to plow through any sense of panic, doubt, or whatever internal or external triggers threaten to hold you back and make your goal feel so required that you feel like you'll die unless you get started on it right this very second.

Lou Adler, a serial entrepreneur, learned this lesson, but almost too late. An easygoing guy, Lou's always got a smile on his face and a good joke at the ready. A natural born storyteller, he especially loves talking about his glory days as a star wide receiver for his college team. "I wasn't just fit back then," Lou says, "I was an Adonis." This fact comforts him in his ongoing struggle to lose the 60 pounds he's picked up since his college days.

"I don't even know how this happened," says Lou about his weight. "I know I'm a type A workaholic entrepreneur, but I'm still an athlete in here," he says as he taps his index finger against his head. "But the rest of me seems to be resigned to being fat. I want to lose the weight. Heck, I start a new diet almost every day. I just can't seem to find the commitment to stick to it."

Lou's big life changer, the moment when his desire to lose the weight became a required goal, came when his doctor diagnosed him with hypertension and type 2 diabetes during a yearly exam. "Reality has finally checked in," Lou told his wife a few hours later when she found him throwing out all the junk food in the house. "This time the diet is no joke. I've got to lose this weight or I could die."

It took the equivalent of a saber-toothed tiger breathing down Lou's neck for him to stop procrastinating and do something about his weight. He was lucky; he got the message, felt the urgency, and lost the weight. But the lesson here is not that you should wait for your equivalent of "Eat even one desert in the next 72 hours and you will suffer a heart attack" to reach that same place of "required" with your own goals. Instead, I want you to learn how to stir up that same kind of urgency about your goals anytime you want to make something happen.

Intellectually, we know we should have a much greater sense of urgency about our goals. We know that putting things off is bad. We overpaid our taxes by hundreds of millions because of procrastination. We wasted almost $7 billion in unused gift cards. In 2010, the Employee Benefit Research Institute's annual retirement survey found that a paltry 16 percent of workers are very confident about having enough money for a comfortable retirement. Self-defeating behavior is generally considered the biggest preventable cause of death, and yet, societally, we postpone quitting smoking, drinking, overeating, and having unsafe sex.

As of right now, tomorrow is officially off-limits. It's time to stop getting tripped up by how your automatic brain views future events (like goals) and pump up the volume on your deliberate brain function to build strong connections to your HARD Goals that make them feel so required that you have no other choice but to start acting on them right here, right now.

## HOW WE VIEW THE FUTURE

We value things in the present more than we value things in the future. This can be a tricky issue, especially since it's not something we typically think about. So I urge you to read that first sentence a few times over and really let it sink in. To better explain how it works, I'll use an approach most people can make an easy connection with: money.

If I were to offer you the choice of $100 right this minute or $100 in one year, which would you pick? The overwhelming majority of people would say, "Gee, thanks. I'll take the money now." There are lots of reasons why this is; you could potentially invest the $100 and in a year have $110. Or, with inflation rates escalating, $100 might only get you $95 worth of stuff in a year, so it's best to grab it now. Could be you have really positive expectations about the future and believe that you'll have so much money in a year that $100 won't seem like as much then as it does right now. Perhaps you're cash strapped and need the money now. Or maybe your picture of what you'd do with the money right now is a lot more vivid than the fuzzy abstract picture of what you'd with the money in the future. And, of course, there's always the thought that you could be dead in a year, so carpe diem.

The most common reason why you wouldn't take the money now is if you don't trust yourself to do something positive with it. You know you won't be making any interest on the money.

And if there's inflation, you'll end up losing money. But even so, taking the year-out offer and treating it like a forced savings plan seems wiser than taking the money now. I've done something like this while cleaning out my briefcase. I'll find a few $20 bills and put them right back thinking, "If I take it out, I'll spend it on something stupid." So I put the money back, make myself forget it's even there, and I figure it'll be a nice financial boon in another six months. Yes, I'm a CEO with a long history of financial success, but I've also got an area of my basement where I stack all the Space Bags and George Foreman Grills that I've bought off late night TV. So perhaps my reasoning to put the money back in my briefcase isn't really that dumb.

The bottom line of all this is that we tend to value the present far more than we do the future. It's just a fact that most people want $100 today rather than $100 in a year. However, what if I offered you a premium? Could I then maybe tempt you to wait and take the money in a year? What if I offered you $110 in one year; would that be enough money to get you to wait? How about $150? Or $200? I can't predict exactly what your number will be, because it'll depend on your current financial situation, other uses you might have for the money, how much risk you think is involved, your expectations about the future, and so on. But you will almost surely have a number, and it will be bigger than $100.

Without getting too mathematical here, you can actually calculate a number called a discount rate. This is basically the extra money you'll need to come up with in the future in order to equal the same value as this year's $100. For instance, If I think getting $150 in one year is equivalent to getting $100 right now, I just divide my one-year increase ($50) by my right-now number ($100), and that gives me a 50 percent discount rate. If I only need $120 in a year, I've got a 20 percent discount rate. If I need $180, I've got an 80 percent discount rate.

Think of it this way: if you buy a CD from your local bank, you're basically saying, "I'll give you $1,000 right now in exchange for $1,010 in one year." Parenthetically, notice how ridiculously low that discount rate is. In fact, as I write this book, CD interest rates paid by banks are around 1 percent. (Obviously the math gets a lot more complicated if you're doing this for multiple years, and so forth, but I'm keeping things simple to illustrate a point.) The higher your discount rate, the less you value the payoff in the future and the more you value the payoff right now.

Now, let's apply the concept of a discount rate to something like dieting. Imagine you're going out to dinner tonight and the waiter brings by a dessert tray with a molten chocolate cake. You want that cake right now, but you also have a diet goal that requires you to reduce your daily food intake by 300 calories. The cake will put you over your calories for today by 800 and put you behind on your weight goal when you check the scale next week.

With this as background, let's analyze the situation. If I eat the cake today, I get to enjoy the sweet chocolate as it oozes into my mouth, creating a biological chain reaction that culminates in a four-alarm pleasure emergency in my brain. That's a good immediate payoff.

But what about my future payoff if I stick to my goal and skip the cake? Well, looking toward the future, I'll probably like the way I look, I'll be emotionally empowered by my self-control, I'll be healthier, and I'll fit into my skinny jeans. These are significantly bigger payoffs than what I stand to gain in the present, but they're occurring at a later time than the enjoyment I'll get from eating the cake right now. If my decision was this:

Option A: Enjoy cake now.
Option B: Look skinny and feel emotionally great tonight.

I'd choose Option B in a heartbeat. But that's not my decision. My decision is more like this:

Option A: Enjoy cake now.
Option B: Look skinny and feel emotionally great in three months (while experiencing cake deprivation in the present).

To the quirky human brain, my future payoff doesn't seem nearly as enticing as what I can get in the present. Granted, my payoff in the future is great (way better than five minutes of cake enjoyment), but I'm mentally discounting that payoff. After all, who knows what the future holds? I could be dead in three months. Maybe I've got some vacation time coming up and rationalize that I'll have plenty of time to diet then, and probably even exercise, too. Maybe in three months science will have discovered a new drug that makes you lose all your excess fat and I won't ever have to think about any of this again.

Whether or not I stick to my diet goal is entirely based on how much I value the present over the future (or how much I discount the future). This will determine whether I eat the cake and get the smaller immediate payoff or forgo the cake and get the bigger future payoff. (In research shorthand this is the Smaller Sooner versus Larger Later choice.)

Each of us has a unique level of bias that makes us value things we could get right now more than the things we could get in the future. In this view, money today is better than money tomorrow, and being a couch potato right now is preferable to training for next year's triathlon. The real issue is just how much more we stand to gain today and to what extent this bias messes with our ability to set and accomplish our goals.

Consider this: roughly 30 percent of adult Americans have high blood pressure (hypertension). And notwithstanding the medical community's efforts to improve recognition and treatment, there is great dissatisfaction with the current rates of controlling this disease. In response, researchers at the Medical University of South Carolina decided to assess to what extent discount rates (how we value the future compared to the present) impacted people's responses to having high blood pressure.[4]

The first thing of note is that the average health discount rates were found to be 43.8 percent per year. Let's think about this for a minute. If we're giving our money to the bank to buy a CD, we only discount the future by about 1 percent (because that's about the interest rate we accept from the bank). But when it comes to high blood pressure (you know, serious health stuff) we devalue the future by nearly 44 percent? No wonder so many people aren't getting the proper treatments right now. They're looking at this and thinking, "Gee, the five minutes I save now by not wasting time checking my blood pressure is worth 43 percent more than the five minutes of extra life I'll get next year by treating this condition."

Further analyses showed that just a 1 percent increase in participants' discount rate increased the likelihood that they would *not* check their blood pressure by 3.5 percent, *not* alter their diet and exercise by 0.6 percent, and *not* follow doctors' treatment plans by 1.6 percent. What's more, the people with the highest discount rates, somewhere between 50 and 57 percent (the folks who don't value the future very highly at all), were almost twice as likely not to change their diet and exercise when they were diagnosed with hypertension.

Bottom line: if you heavily discount the future (you value the present a lot more than the future), you're a lot less likely to be moved by the prospect of achieving great results in the future. I could tell you that following your doctor's orders and treating your high blood pressure will add time to your life. But if you don't value that future time very much (if you discount it heavily), you're not likely to be swayed by my argument.

You might be tempted to think that this only applies to goals where you pay a price right now (like taking blood pressure medication, exercising, or giving up chocolate cake) and you don't get any benefits until much later (like good health, skinny jeans, and the like). But it turns out it's not just difficult goals that get heavily discounted. The problem of future discounting also hurts enjoyable experiences.

In a terrific study on sightseeing, researchers at UCLA and UC San Diego surveyed people who either lived in or were visiting Chicago, London, or Dallas.[5] The study asked a series of questions, such as how long the person had been in that city and which major landmarks he or she had visited. Among the findings were that the average two-week visitor visits 4.4 landmarks, while the average resident living in the city for up to one year only sees 3.1 landmarks. In other words, brief tourists see about 42 percent more landmarks than residents do. Additionally, the average three-week visitor sees 5.5 landmarks, which is 17 percent more than the 4.7 landmarks visited by residents who have lived in that city for three or more years.

What was even more amazing was that for residents, 60 percent of their visits to major local landmarks happened with out-of-town guests. So even the visits they did make were largely driven by brief tourists. (I can personally relate to this last point.

While I grew up in Buffalo, I probably never would have visited Niagara Falls had it not been the most requested destination for all the out-of-town relatives.)

So how exactly does all this relate to discounting of the future? Well, here's the kicker. The folks who resided in the cities didn't evenly space their visits throughout their tenure living there. The scientists contacted people who had moved out of Chicago and put them through a similar battery of questions. But this time, they focused on the timing of their visits to the landmarks. These former residents had lived in Chicago for an average of three years, and 40 percent of the visits they made to landmarks occurred within the last six months of their time there. And 18 percent of their visits actually occurred in their last two weeks!

Visiting major landmarks is supposed to be fun. When you're in Chicago, trips to the Field Museum, Willis Tower (formerly called the Sears Tower), or the architectural riverboat tour are pretty enjoyable. And yet, without a sense of urgency (such as short-term tourists feel), people delay and delay. When we discount the future we believe the benefits we'll get in the future pale in comparison to any benefits we'll get from doing whatever we happen to be doing right at the moment. The psychological calculator in our brains basically says, "Eh, the discounted payoff's just not big enough to stop what I'm doing and visit the Willis Tower. I can always do that later (next month, next year)."

There's another related psychological phenomenon taking place here as well: people seriously overestimate how much free time they'll have in the future. This sounds something like, "Well, I'm swamped right now, but in a few months I'll have lots more time." On the flip side, to someone visiting a city for two weeks, the future is only two weeks. Brief visitors are not likely to discount the future enjoyment they'll get from those landmarks by very much. And their estimate of future free time is pretty much moot (again, the future is only two weeks).

The same researchers also looked at how future discounting affects gift certificate use. In one study, gift certificates to a gourmet French pastry café with either a three-week or two-month expiration date were given to study participants. Not surprisingly (given what we've just learned), the people who got the two-month expiration were much more likely to believe they wouldn't have any trouble using the gift certificate before it expired. In fact, 68 percent of the two-month expiration recipients expected they would use it compared to only 50 percent of the three-week expiration group. But when it came to actual usage, 31 percent of the three-week recipients actually redeemed their gift certificates, while a paltry 6 percent of the two-month crowd actually redeemed their certificates.

Remember, people generally overestimate their future free time, so they postpone things (even good things) until that future time. There's simply no sense of urgency, and this translates directly into our goals. Our future time is so heavily discounted (relative to the payoffs we could be getting right this very minute) that we simply don't see the future payoffs as really being worth that much.

---

## WHAT CAN WE DO ABOUT THIS?

So the big question becomes, what can we do about this? Well, let's remember something. While there are exceptions, challenging goals often follow a very basic form: exert some effort now and get some benefit in the future. So forgo desert tonight, be skinny in three months. Curb your impulse spending now, have more retirement money in a year. Train now, run in the Olympics in four years. Attend that management course now, get a promotion at your next annual review. Get your employees working on a new strategy now, generate more sales next quarter.

By itself that doesn't seem like a big problem; it's quite OK that most goals require some immediate costs but don't offer their benefits until the future. After all, if I said to you, "Give up $100 now and get $170 in one year," you might take the deal. Really challenging goals will always have some costs, but even outstanding costs are usually outweighed by the benefits.

The problem isn't that our benefits aren't big enough. We like the thought of what we stand to gain by seeing our goals through, even when we know we're not going to get it right now. But we don't stand a chance at getting it at all if our brains tell us the future just ain't worth it and right now is way more important. For instance, consider the number of people who rationalize that it's better to save five minutes of time now by not checking their blood pressure—even in the face of life-threatening hypertension. Even the most enticing potential benefits (like having a long and healthy life rather than a painful and imminent death) aren't going to be enough to lure us into taking action now if the future holds little to no value to us.

And the further you move into the future, the worse it gets. If your goal is: do 500 sit-ups today and have killer washboard abs by tomorrow, you'd probably be on it in a heartbeat. But how many HARD Goals can deliver a return that quickly? The fact is, you have to diet (sensibly) for several months to maybe lose 30 pounds. If even the thought of this sets off an automatic reaction in you that says, "Forget it, half a year of torture for some time in the future I can't even fathom is stupid; I'm gonna go get some hot wings," you're in the norm. Your brain is doing its thing and telling you the future is less important than right now, benefits be damned.

If you only discount the future by 10 percent, you have a chance. You'll probably take my offer to give up $100 today and get $170 next year, or give the diet a go, or take the risk and start a business. Whatever your goal is. But if you're discounting your future payoffs by 80 percent, then the $170 you'll get next year is only worth $94 today, and there's no way you'll take my offer. Same goes for the diet and everything else. Unfortunately, most of us fall into the high discount rate category.

The good news is that we can combat the problem. It just requires taking some deliberate steps (tricking the brain, really) to diminish the impact of our discount rates. Our minds may basically be wired to apply this discounting formula to all our decisions, but we can manipulate that formula to our advantage by tweaking how we structure the inputs and outputs. This allows us to outflank our own brains, thus opening the floodgates to a sense of urgency about our goals (they become required). Following are six great ways to do this.

## Trick 1: Put Your Present Costs into the Future

One way to cut down on your high discount rate is to move some of the immediate costs of your goal into the future. You'll still be dealing with discounting the future benefits of your goals (it's just what we do), but by discounting some of the future costs you can shift the balance a bit. Often just this alone is enough to radically alter the mental equation in favor of your goal.

One example of how this is done is the brainchild of one of the great minds in behavioral economics, University of Chicago

Professor Richard Thaler. A few years ago Thaler, along with his frequent collaborator, Professor Shlomo Benartzi, pioneered a savings program called Save More Tomorrow.[6]

We all know that people don't save enough for retirement (remember the statistic shared earlier where only 16 percent of workers feel confident about their retirement savings?). But people also aren't particularly willing to reduce their take-home pay and stick the money in a retirement savings account. The Save More Tomorrow plan asks people to save more, but not today.

Participants in the plan commit to increasing their savings rate as they get pay raises. This way, they never see their take-home pay decline; it just doesn't go up as much. Moving some of the present costs of saving into the future makes the goal of saving money seem appealing to folks who might not consider a more traditional savings plan (the people who have a high discount rate for the future).

The plan proved to be a startling success. At the manufacturing company where the plan was first pioneered, almost 90 percent of employees sat down with a financial consultant who basically told them (no surprise) that they needed to save more. About a quarter of folks took the advice and increased their savings. The rest, unwilling to cut their current take-home pay, were offered the Save More Tomorrow plan. Those who joined committed to increase their savings by 3 percent every time they got a pay raise (which were running about 3.25 to 3.5 percent at the time).

Over a three-year period, the 10 percent or so of people who never met with the financial consultant at all saved a fairly steady 6 percent. The group who met with the consultant and took his advice to increase their savings went from saving about 4 percent to about 9 percent. And the Save More Tomorrow crowd? They started out pretty low, saving only 3.5 percent. But three and a half years later, their savings rate had just about quadrupled to a whopping 13.6 percent. Parenthetically, given its success, and the successful psychology behind it, this kind of plan is becoming increasingly popular. A study in 2007 found that almost 40 percent of large companies offered some kind of future escalation plan.

So why is a plan like this so effective? Well, instead of having a situation in which you incur huge undiscounted costs right now and heavily discounted benefits at some point in the future, this plan basically syncs up the costs and benefits. It pushes your costs out into your highly discounted future where they don't seem that big anymore. It's a very clever trick to play on your brain, and the results speak for themselves.

## Trick 2: Put Your Future Benefits into the Present

In Trick 1 we put some of the present costs of a goal into the future to help us devalue our costs and thus make the benefits look more attractive. Trick 2 is the converse of that, where you bring some of the future benefits of your goal into the here-and-now. This way your brain won't discount the benefits and your goal will look a lot more attractive right now, inspiring a sense of urgency to get going on it.

Let's look at another type of savings plan that offsets the future benefits of saving by offering some immediate benefit. One group of people that tends to put a high discount on the future (especially when it comes to money) is those in a lower income bracket. It's been found that a lot of these folks feel like they're more likely to become rich through winning the lottery than through savings. Hence, a frightening number of people who fall into this category don't even have a simple checking or savings account. In response to this, there are now savings plans in which you put money into an account, and in doing so get entered into a lottery-like drawing for prizes, cash, and so forth. Because the monthly lottery drawing is in present time, it lessens the focus on the faraway (and less tempting) benefit of saving money. Simply put, to those who discount the future benefit of saving money, it brings some immediate reward and gets them on board with saving.

Premium Bonds in Britain are an example of an investment where, instead of interest payments, investors have the chance to win tax-free prizes. Anyone who invests in Premium Bonds is allocated a series of numbers, one for each £1 invested. The minimum purchase is £100, which provides 100 Bond numbers and, therefore, 100 chances of winning a prize. Prizes range from two £1 million prizes to more than a million £50 prizes. There are currently 23 million bondholders holding £26 billion worth of Premium Bonds. The marketing pitch on the Premium Bond website is, "They are a fun, yet serious way of saving, combining the chance of winning tax-free prizes with the peace of mind that comes from knowing your capital is 100 percent secure."

I'm not going to tell you that this is a better investment than a mutual fund or anything that generates positive interest or returns. But if you've got a high discount rate on your goal (and if you've ever smoked, overeaten, wasted money, and so forth, you might have a very high discount rate, at least for that issue), then this is one way of putting some otherwise future benefits in the here-and-now.

When Carl (I'm omitting his last name because he's an engineer for a government agency) set a goal to nab a promotion at work, he knew it was going to be a tough challenge. Meeting his goal meant learning new skills, which translated into night classes. Weekend time would have to be set aside for studying, and he was going to have to devote more weekday hours to the job. All this meant less time at home with his wife and three-year-old son, and pretty much no time (at least for a while) to devote to fun things like friends and hobbies.

It's not that Carl doesn't want the future payoff of his intended goal. He and his wife have been talking about having a second child, and the pay raise that comes with the promotion will make it a lot easier to do. In fact, growing his family is Carl's primary heartfelt motivator behind his goal. But even so, he feels a certain level of dread about the coming months, of all he is going to have to give up. And he feels anxious that he might not have what it takes to pull it off.

To help stay motivated and on track for his HARD Goal, Carl took a hard look at the future benefits he stood to gain to see what he might be able to move into the present. While he and his wife made a firm resolve of "no new baby until there is more money," they could still stir up some excitement about growing their family. Obviously, practicing for that day is a benefit most of us can appreciate. Carl also decided to start the nursery room as a way of bringing into the present some of the future benefits. "Just working on the room reminds me of why I am pushing myself so hard right now," Carl says. "As my wife and I paint and paper, we feel excited about the prospect of having a baby. We might not be able to do it today, but we're keeping the excitement alive, and that really helps me get up every day and do what I have to do."

## Trick 3: Make Your Benefits Sound Better

One of the mental incongruities people often have is to view costs in very concrete terms and benefits in very abstract terms (this concept was introduced back in the "Animated" chapter).

If I were to describe the costs of my current diet, I could make a very concrete list a mile long: I can't eat three slices of pizza or a bucket of wings, gotta give up molten chocolate cake, no more dinners out at Ray's, can't eat fried green tomatoes with the horseradish cream sauce, I'll get hunger pangs in the evening, and on and on. Notice how specific, concrete, and long that list is.

Now, if I were to forget all I know about HARD Goals and describe the benefits of my diet, the list might sound something like this: I'll be skinny, I'll feel better about myself, I'll live longer and be healthier. Notice how that benefits list is shorter and way more abstract than the costs list? If you remember back to the "Animated" chapter where I shared with you how poor our recall is for abstract words, it's no wonder the benefits appear meager in comparison to the costs.

By using some of the techniques we learned in the "Animated" chapter, we can go through our future benefits and make them a lot more concrete. Instead of saying, "I'll be skinny" we could say, "I'll wear those dark blue jeans that I haven't worn in eight years, and I'll pair them with that slim-fitting shirt I ordered online in a size too small and thus haven't yet been able to wear." If you're CEO of a hospital, instead of saying, "We're going to a create a culture that values patient safety," you could say, "We're going to report every single mistake that could have potentially harmed a patient, even if it didn't actually harm the patient, and within 72 hours we're going to learn at least two correctable lessons and implement a solution within 96 hours after that so that every doctor and nurse knows with certainty that patient safety is our number one priority." You'll want to literally detail every single benefit you'll get from achieving this goal, and, using the techniques I gave in the "Animated" chapter, make sure it's concrete, visual, animated, and so forth.

## Trick 4: Minimize Your Costs

Of course, it's always good if you can just get your brain to stop perseverating about all the costs you're going to incur to achieve a goal. But turning off your brain is hard to do. Quick, don't think about a pink elephant—whatever you do, don't you dare picture a pink elephant standing in the middle of your room! Hard, right? Think of it like this: I don't particularly like heights, so if I were high up on a ledge, I really wouldn't want to look down. But if someone says to me, "Don't look down," of course I'm going to look down. Why? Because before I can negate a thought (do *not* look down), I first have to access that thought (look down). So I think, *Look down, no wait, I'm supposed to negate that thought, crap, it's too late, I just looked down . . . Arrggh!*

I'm not going to tell you to try and deny that your goals have some associated costs (I'll never tell you not to look down). Instead, I'm going to tell you to "look up"—to take your costs and recast every one of them as a benefit. Let's start simply with the diet goal, which on some level most of us can connect with. Say tonight you're going out to dinner, and you make a resolve to forgo the molten chocolate cake. What are the costs of that? One easy cost is that you have to formally turn away the cake; you have to incur the emotional pain of saying no. Now, does that cost have any upside? Is there any way you can benefit from this act of saying no?

Well, if it were me, here's what I'd say. First, passing on the cake shows I've got mental toughness. I read an interview with Lance Armstrong a while back in which he basically said he loves it when the ride turns tough. When it's a festival of pain he's going to win every time because he's tougher, with a better tolerance for pain than anyone else. So I'm kind of like Lance Armstrong here, and how cool is that?

Another benefit is that this proves that I am totally committed to my weight-loss goal. Turning down the cake shows

I'm in it for the long haul; I'm absolutely going to hit my goal. And remember that one of the factors that cause our discount rates to be so high is that we feel the future is highly uncertain. So when you combat uncertainty with certainty, your discount rate declines, future benefits seem more appealing, and so on. Or to put it another way: "ain't nothin' gonna breaka my stride, nobody gonna slow me down, oh no . . ."

There are two very good questions you can ask yourself in order to reframe a cost as a benefit. The first is, What will I learn from this? And the second, How does the cost demonstrate my commitment to an even bigger goal? Let's take a look:

### What Will I Learn from This?

One of our studies on goals found that people really like to learn, that gaining new knowledge or skills is an incredibly rewarding benefit in its own right. We'll go deeper into this in the "Difficult" chapter, but right now I want to introduce some results from when we looked at employees who will have to learn new skills to accomplish their work goals.

Those who will have to learn new skills are:

- Twenty-two times more likely to say, "I would like to spend my career at this organization."
- Seventeen times more likely to say, "I recommend my boss to others as a great person to work for."
- Twenty-one times more likely to say, "I recommend this organization to others as a great place for people to work."

When you can evaluate a tough goal and say, "You know what, that was really hard, but wow, did I learn a lot of new skills," you're significantly more likely to walk away from that challenge with a sense of empowerment and deepened commitment to your bigger goals. For example, when I forgo the cake, I'm learning all sorts of new skills. I'm learning to estimate calories, I'm learning to read my body's signals to distinguish between mental feelings of hunger and an actual physical need for calories, I'm learning to make my body more efficient, I'm learning to control my thoughts and desires (like a Jedi master), I'm learning clever ways to satiate my sweet tooth through lower-calorie alternatives like fruit, and lots more.

On the career path to management jobs, it's generally accepted that there are some stepping-stones that make the career path a little easier. Doing strategy consulting, turnaround restructuring (where I began my career), or venture capital, just to name a few, are all seen as pretty good places to launch a management career. Why? Because the learning curve is intense, and every company wants to hire people that have a track record of learning a lot, very quickly, and under intense pressure. In a way, the costs you're incurring with these goals aren't really costs; they're more like investments in building a better, faster, smarter, tougher you.

When Quinn Taylor decided to finally get organized, it seemed like the hardest goal she had ever set for herself. "Work, personal life, my kids, the house, it's all a mess," she admitted. "But I knew if I kept on going this way I'd self-destruct. I've had too many narrow misses where my mess has almost gotten me in a lot trouble."

Sticking to her goal wasn't easy. From the very start Quinn had a mad desire to drop it all and run. "I kept trying to tell myself it was just a little chaos, nothing that was going to kill me," she said. "So I had to find a way to stay plugged in to my goal, so every day I would take on a piece of my mess and make it better."

What ended up hooking Quinn was all she started to learn about herself once she made the commitment to really dig in and clean up the chaos. "I never really thought before about why I am addicted to clutter—both tangible and mental," said Quinn. "It's just one more way for me to avoid being truly present. My mess has made me miss out on a lot of good stuff in life, like really important moments with my kids. I'm always scrambling last minute to find this, do that, fix this. It takes a lot of energy. It's negatively impacted not just my life, but also my family. We're all a lot happier these days."

Quinn learned something else about herself too, something that will help her be a better goal setter in the future. "I think the most outstanding thing that came of getting organized was that I did it. I really didn't think I could, but I did. It wasn't easy, but I pushed through and was successful. I feel so much more confident now about other stuff I want to tackle—even bigger goals. I learned that I don't have to allow my brain to switch over to 'that's impossible' mode anymore when I get an idea. Instead, I think, 'Wow, I could actually do that.' It's really empowering."

### How Does the Cost Demonstrate My Commitment to a Larger Goal?

It's important to remember that goals aren't usually an all-or-nothing phenomenon. You can achieve small parts of a bigger goal (like forgoing the cake tonight is a small part of a larger weight-loss goal). But how we view our accomplishments on those small parts can impact our commitment to the larger goal.

Some recent research suggests that when people view their accomplishment on the small part as a distinct event that's separate from the bigger goal, it actually undercuts their motivation to keep working toward that bigger goal. It's like their brain says, "Whew, that was tough, but at least it's over now and I can just stop working." But when they view the small accomplishment as a demonstration of their commitment to a larger goal, well, not surprisingly, they get even more committed to the bigger goal. So whenever you have these accomplishments that are smaller parts of a bigger goal, always make sure you tell yourself how this demonstrates your commitment to the bigger goal.

Howie Peirce was in the audience of one of my speeches. After a quick chat (and a signed book) he told me, "I just have a terrible time getting things done. I am the king of procrastination." He said it with a smile, but if you talk to him for a few minutes you'll inevitably hear him admit he's not really laughing. "So I set a HARD Goal to start seeing my stuff through," Howie said, "starting with my goal to see things through!"

Not every day is flawless for Howie. "I struggle some days, I'm not going to lie," he says. "But I take each day as a new challenge. Like today, my boss asked me to update part of our quarterly financials spreadsheet. No big deal, but typically I would get distracted by something and forget to close the loop and let everyone else on the team know when it was done, stuff like that. But not today. I saw my task out through to the end. It actually feels good to know I'm not hanging one of my teammates out to dry with version control problems or bad data on that report."

Howie's goal is a lifelong endeavor, just like Quinn's goal to be organized. For both of them, if they don't view their daily efforts to meet their goal as a commitment to the larger goal, it would be too easy to become discouraged, drop out, and fail.

## Trick 5: Attack Your Discount Rate Directly

People often ask me whether it's possible to just attack your discount rate directly. After all, if that's the real problem, why not just make it lower? Well, our individual discount rates are functions of how we view the world, the future, our goals, our abilities, our sense of time, and much more. Our discount rate is a reflection of our deepest personality traits. So, all in all, it's a hard thing to change. However, all is not lost because there is something we can do.

On the whole, our discount rates reflect our feelings but often don't reflect reality. I might choose to smoke cigarettes and eat that cake because I really discount/devalue the future. After all, I could get hit by a bus next month, so to heck with it, carpe diem. Or I just feel invincible, which also completely skews my discount rate and sense of the future. But the reality is that I'm not likely to get hit by a bus, nor am I likely to be invincible. It's a lot more likely that I'll get some really painful disease and suffer for a long time; heart attacks and lung cancer aren't fun diseases. The trouble is that we do a lot of "black-and-white thinking," and it very rarely corresponds with reality.

So here's what you can do: benchmark yourself. Go out and find people similar to yourself; get a decent-sized pool of comparisons and track their ups and downs, behaviors, outcomes, goals, successes, failures, and so on. (If you're thinking that social media like Facebook and Twitter are good for this, you're right.) You basically need a pool of comparison data points to get a better sense of what the future really looks like. And, as you watch these folks, start adjusting your discount rate. If none of them got hit by a bus, then maybe you'll learn something about the statistical likelihood of that happening. If two of them lose their jobs, maybe that will adjust your discount rate for retirement planning. And if you're comparing yourself to a bunch of CEOs and 80 percent of their companies are struggling to grow, then perhaps that will impact how you assess the costs and benefits of your goals.

## Trick 6: Limit Your Choices

There's one final technique to outflank your brain and create a much more deeply felt sense of requirement for your goals. It's to limit the number of alternatives you have competing with your goals. It's become an accepted truism that more choice is always better. But the truth is that too many choices can actually hamper our ability to achieve our goals. When we go to that restaurant, we want to be able to decide what we want based on our feelings in that moment; we like to keep our options open. But when we're in that moment, staring at all those dessert choices, we can become mentally overloaded, lose focus, and start making selections that undercut our goals. (If you stare at that almost limitless dessert tray without a clear plan, bad things will happen.)

Researchers at Columbia and Stanford, led by Sheena S. Iyengar and Mark R. Lepper, have made some fascinating discoveries about how much choice is too much.[7] In one study, the researchers set up displays of gourmet jams in a specialty grocery store. In one display, customers passing by could taste 24 different flavored jams, while in another display there was only the option of tasting 6 different flavored jams.

Well, more choices are better, right? Initially the customers thought so, as 60 percent of passersby stopped at the display with 24 jams and only 40 percent of passersby stopped at the 6-jam display. But that's where having a lot of choices stopped being a good thing. Out of all the customers that stopped at the 24-jam tasting display, only 3 percent actually ended up buying a jam. But when customers stopped at the 6-jam display, 30 percent ended up buying a jam. That's a 10 times better customer conversion rate, and it comes from offering fewer choices, not more.

Sheena Iyengar has conducted similar research looking at 401(k) plan participation.[8] Of course, companies think that people want lots of choices, so when they offer a 401(k) plan, they give employees lots of different investment choices to pick from. But like the jam study, when a company offers more choices of investment funds, employee participation in the 401(k) plan decreases. For example, if a 401(k) plan only offered two funds to invest in, employee participation rates could hit as high as 75 percent. But when a 401(k) plan offered 59 different funds to choose from, employee participation rates dropped to about 60 percent. In fact, for every additional 10 investment fund choices the company provided, employee participation rates would decline as much as 2 percent.

Parenthetically, have you ever wondered why Amazon.com makes "recommendations" for you? (If you buy enough stuff from them, they'll start looking at your past purchases and using those to recommend other products that you're statistically likely to enjoy.) Of course, Amazon wants to be helpful. But more fundamentally, they're trying to limit your choices (albeit in a very nice and helpful way). They know that if you see too many options on a page, you won't end up buying any of them. But if they can limit your choices to just a few recommendations, you're way more likely to actually buy one of them.

I should note that in studies, people initially said they wanted more choices. But when they got more choices, they ended up being less satisfied with their purchases and experienced much more regret. By contrast, people that were offered fewer choices were significantly happier, experienced less regret, and in the case of the first study I mentioned, were 10 times more likely to buy something.

Remember that our brains are always calculating costs and benefits. When we see too many choices, our brains get overwhelmed and crash like a cheap laptop. So before you go into a situation laden with choices, narrow your options and then pick one. In the studies I mentioned, good outcomes were those where people made a purchase or chose a retirement plan. When it comes to goals, good outcomes are those where you stick to your goals, and bad outcomes are those where you do something clearly incongruous with those ends.

So narrow your choices, and you'll have a much better chance of sticking to your goals. Read the restaurant's menu before you go out to dinner so you don't get overwhelmed by the dessert tray and end up gorging on that chocolate cake and spending the subsequent hours in a cycle of self-recrimination. Plan your trips to the gym well before you have that long day at work and then don't feel like going. Don't buy your company that online training library that has 300 different course titles and just throw it out there expecting your employees will initiate an educational binge; pick a narrow menu of specific courses you want everyone to complete.

Finally, anytime you have a deadline on any type of goal, don't give yourself too many choices. In one study, researchers Dan Ariely (author of the terrific book *Predictably Irrational*) and Klaus Wertenbroch analyzed how people set their own deadlines in a class and what happened to their grades when they did so.[9] This was an executive education class at MIT (in other words, not a freshman class but rather seasoned professionals paying a lot of money for some high-level thinking). For this particular class, students were assigned to write three papers. In one group, they were given evenly spaced deadlines (one paper due after each third of the class). The other group could set their own deadlines. For example, they could choose to make all three papers due on the very last day (the only caveat was that these deadlines had to be selected up front and they were binding). Now rationally, you'd want as much time as possible (in other words, to make all three papers due on the last day of class) because you would have learned more in the class, maybe you'd find synergy between the papers, and so on. But it didn't really work out that way.

Students who were given the evenly spaced deadlines had better grades than those who chose their own deadlines (so much for free choice always being better). But another interesting factor was that the people who chose their own deadlines, but gave themselves evenly spaced deadlines (similar to the no-choice crowd) had grades that were basically indistinguishable from the no-choice crowd (and better than the people who made all three papers due on the last day). So the lesson seems to be that when you take away some of your choices, structure your thinking, and force yourself into an arbitrary sense of urgency, you'll perform better.

## ANIMATED AND REQUIRED ARE GREAT FRIENDS

The endowment effect is one of my favorite psychological biases. Discovered by Richard Thaler, and inspired by Amos Tversky and Daniel Kahneman, it basically says that people place a higher value on objects they own than on objects they do not own. For example, let's say you owned a plain red ceramic coffee mug and I wanted to buy it from you. There's a good chance, following a number of actual experiments on this topic, you would say to me, "I won't sell this mug of mine for less than $7." However, if you went into a store to buy the same exact coffee mug, there's a good chance you wouldn't pay more than $3 for it. How do you explain the discrepancy? We value things that we own more than things we don't yet own.

One of my favorite experiments on this topic involved pizza (and you already know about my heartfelt connection to pizza). Irwin Levin, from the University of Iowa, and Marco Lauriola, from the University of Rome "La Sapienza" in Italy, wanted to see how the endowment effect impacted the purchase of pizza.[10] College students in Iowa and Italy were given the task of building their own pizza by selecting from a menu of 12 ingredients (if all experiments were like this, I'd make my next career being a permanent research subject).

In the America version, the students were divided into two groups: an Adding Condition or a Subtracting Condition. In the Adding Condition, subjects started with a description of a "basic" cheese pizza with no extra ingredients and were asked to select additional toppings like mushrooms, peppers, pineapple, pepperoni, and so forth for 50 cents each. In the Subtracting Condition, subjects started with a "super" pizza with all 12 ingredients and were told that the price would be reduced by 50 cents for each topping they subtracted. Both groups were told that they should add or delete as many ingredients as they wanted until they got their preferred pizza. The Italian version of the experiment was basically the same, but some ingredients were adapted to Italian tastes (pepperoni and pineapple were replaced by Italian hot sausage and Italian vegetables) and the Italian students were also asked to choose ingredients for a salad. (Salad, huh? There's probably some kind of a healthy lifestyle lesson in there somewhere.)

Now the Subtracting Condition is kind of like taking ownership of the pizza. You've mentally pictured this pizza with all of its ingredients; as far as your brain is concerned, that's your pizza right there. If somebody tried to take those ingredients away, your brain would be like, "Hey, those are my peppers, pepperoni, and sausage!" Even if you don't really love peppers or sausage, your brain is saying, "Those are mine, I own them," and thus is a lot less willing to let them go. But in the Adding Condition, all you really own is the basic cheese pizza. Those extra ingredients are not mentally owned by your brain, you haven't pictured them on your pizza yet, so you just don't care nearly as much if they end up on your pizza or not.

The experiment confirmed this thinking. In Iowa, students in the Adding Condition only ended up with 2.7 ingredients on average. But the Subtracting Condition students, who mentally owned those ingredients and thus were much less willing to give them up, averaged about 5.3 ingredients. If you started with the "super" loaded pizza and had to subtract ingredients, you would spend about $1.29 more for your pizza than people who started with just a cheese pizza. The Italian experiment showed the same thing, and even on their salad choices, if they started with the loaded salad they ended up with twice as many toppings. (Yes, every salesperson and marketer on the planet should be glued to this page right now.)

So, what does this all mean? If you take the lessons of the "Animated" chapter—animating and visualizing your goal, making it come alive in your head—it's a lot like the Subtracting Condition in the pizza experiment. If you take mental ownership of this goal in your mind's eye—it's yours, you own it—then in response to any activity that tries to steal that goal from you (whether it's procrastination or something conflicting), your brain is going to say, "I want my damn goal, get your butt into gear! Stop doing that other thing that's stealing time away from my goal and get moving!"

So one way to make your goal really required is to make it animated. When you bring the future into the present with an incredibly vivid picture of your goal, your brain takes ownership of it; it wants it right here, right now. It's like outflanking the discounting of the future your brain would normally do. And, just as with the pizza ingredients, your brain is going to be willing to pay more to keep possession of that goal. Your brain can touch, smell, feel, and taste that goal in your mental picture, and now it's willing to pay a much steeper price to keep it. If you say to your brain, "Sorry, I was just teasing you with that vivid picture, we're not anywhere near the goal yet," your brain is going to say back to you, "Then get off your butt and start working on that goal, because I tasted that pizza with peppers and sausage, and now I want more."

## SUMMARY

Procrastination is the number one killer of HARD Goals. But that doesn't mean your goals have to be its next victim. You can use the tricks described in this chapter to alter how you view and value your future payoffs so they become more attractive than what the status quo is offering today. You can intentionally move some of the immediate costs of your goal into the future in order to sync up the costs and benefits. Or, conversely, you can bring some of your goal's future benefits into the present. Both will make your goal look a whole lot more attractive and amp up your urgency to get going on it now.

It's easy to consider all the things you'll have to sacrifice in order to achieve your goal, and that kind of list can be a real downer. But you can overcome that negativity with another kind of list—one that details the specific and concrete ways in which your goal is going to make your life a much better place to be. And what about directly attacking how you discount the value of the future? Forget what you've heard about not comparing yourself to others—go ahead and do it. With a little bit of benchmarking, you can more accurately recalculate your discount rate and make it easier to get started on that goal of yours today. Also, limit your choices, make it easier on yourself to choose a goal. And lastly, take mental ownership of your goal. Once it's gotten a taste, your brain will never let it go.

Get more examples and tools at hardgoals.com.

# 4

# Difficult

Back in the Introduction I asked you to complete a short exercise that asked you to name the most significant and meaningful accomplishments in your life—achievements that may have been professional or personal, or whatever. For example, "When I started a new business," "The day I ran the Boston Marathon (and all the training that led up to it)," "Standing in the starting gate at the Olympics," "That breakthrough product I invented," "When I nursed my sick child back to health," or "When I got my college degree." Remember, it's no one's call but yours to name the victories that have been the most important to you.

Now I want you to take whatever response you gave and consider the following:

- Were those accomplishments easy or hard to achieve?
- Did I exert a little or a lot of effort?

- Did I already know everything I needed to know when I started out, or did I have to learn new skills in order to succeed?
- Was I completely worry free, or did I have a few doubts or even some nervousness along the way?
- Was I totally relaxed throughout the process, or did I get "amped up" (excited, alert, elevated heart rate, and the like)?

So what did you just learn about yourself and your history with HARD Goals? Personally, every noteworthy accomplishment I've ever had was difficult. It was hard to do, demanded a lot of effort, I had to learn new stuff, boy did I have moments of worry, and yeah, I was totally amped up, so much so that all that other stuff wasn't nearly as threatening as it could have been. And I've got a point of reference (as do you), because obviously I've done millions of things that weren't difficult (like eating pizza or reading a book). I've also done lots of really difficult things that weren't particularly noteworthy (like watching any movie with Ben Affleck in it). But generally, when I look at my biggest and most meaningful accomplishments, every one of them required some serious work on my part.

I've asked these same questions of tens of thousands of people, whether in our formal studies or just polling audience members at my speaking engagements. And what I can tell you is that overwhelmingly, most people's greatest accomplishments were difficult, required lots of effort, depended upon learning new skills, caused some nervousness, and made their doers feel "amped up" and excited. Just like mine.

Now that we know our greatest accomplishments require effort, learning, and so on, let's take this exercise one step further. Using those same significant and meaningful accomplishments, ask yourself these questions:

- Did my accomplishments leave me feeling indifferent or beaming with pride?
- If I felt pride, was it fleeting, or do I still feel a sense of pride months, or even years, later?
- Was each accomplishment just a one-time deal, or do I feel like I'm a better person (or parent, professional, and so on) because of everything I learned and accomplished as a result of it?

Granted, I have studied tens of thousands of people, but even if I hadn't, my own personal experience tells me that my most significant accomplishments left me beaming with pride, even years later. I'm also a better person, parent, husband, and CEO for having accomplished every one of my HARD Goals, no matter how difficult they were to achieve. But even though a goal was tough, a genuine challenge, I don't feel any regret (like I do about watching those Ben Affleck movies). I feel proud, tough, confident, and significantly more competent. Am I ever going to run an Olympic marathon? Probably not; innate talent does have at least a little mediating role to play here. But I will carry my marathon with me, slow though it was, every day for the rest of my life.

I feel pretty confident when I say that that you probably feel the same way. Because the results of every study we do, the responses of every audience I ask, indicate the same thing. It's the rare person who can't say, "My biggest achievements are among my greatest sources of pride and self-respect, no matter how long ago they occurred, and I'm a better person for having accomplished them."

I hope, like me, that you find this pretty heartening evidence. You and I have done big things before, and even though they were tough, we're both glad we did them. We're stronger, smarter, better, and more fulfilled for having made those journeys. By the way, that's what this whole book is about: improving our goal-setting tool kit so we can go tackle lots more of those really big challenges and be even more accomplished and fulfilled as a result. And this chapter in particular is going to help you set goals that are difficult enough to bring out your very best.

## WE HAVE THE NATURAL ABILITY TO ACHIEVE REMARKABLY DIFFICULT GOALS

Remember Lyle, the four-time Olympian I mentioned earlier? He knew from a very early age that he would one day make the Olympic cut. "When I was 15 the national team came to my little town to train," Lyle says. "One of the athletes asked me if I wanted to ski with the team. Of course I said yes. They were probably just taking a rest day, skiing slowly, but I didn't know that then. I was saying to myself, 'Hey, I can do anything these guys can do. I'm just like them.' My self-image was ratcheting up and up. It was huge. I went home that night and made an unwavering commitment to become an Olympic athlete." And as we know, Lyle succeeded in making that goal a reality, four times over.

By now you may have recognized an underlying theme throughout everything you've read thus far. I believe, and so do lots of other experts, that the overwhelming majority of human beings have tremendous untapped potential. That's why HARD Goals work so well; they are designed to help unleash the depth of great possibility that already exists inside of you. OK, so maybe you're not going to be an Olympic skier like Lyle, or a billionaire, CEO, supermodel, or Nobel laureate. But let me first say that a good deal of what determines our end results is our desire for those results, and not everyone wants to be those things. But that doesn't mean each of us doesn't have perfectly viable HARD Goals that we do wish to attain.

Second, even if we're not aiming for the Olympics, virtually all of us can radically improve our financial position, run a marathon, advance our career, be healthier, and strengthen our intellect. With a little nod to the armed forces here, every one of us can maximize our human potential (you know, be all we can be).

The flip side of this idea is another major theme you've no doubt noticed running through this book: when people underperform their potential, it's usually more an issue of motivation than of innate talent. That's really important, so let me repeat it: we've generally got the innate talent we need to accomplish remarkably difficult goals. And if we're not accomplishing those difficult goals, it's usually not for lack of talent; it's for lack of motivation.

This is why I get a cranky when I hear the "it's all genetic" crowd fatalistically tell us that our lives are predetermined by our DNA (if you don't have the natural talent, oh well, don't waste your energy trying). Or when I hear the "happiness" crowd say that the surest path to fulfillment is to stop trying so hard, to just sit back and be thankful for what's right in front of us.

I'll tell you what I'm thankful for: I'm thankful that Thomas Jefferson, Abraham Lincoln, John F. Kennedy, Martin Luther King Jr., Mahatma Gandhi, and Mother Teresa, among others, didn't buy into any of those crazy arguments. I'm thankful that each one of them was willing to push past what's easy in order to achieve some exceptionally difficult goals. Otherwise they wouldn't have founded a country, put a man on the moon, liberated a nation, freed a people, and so on.

Rather than use a study to prove my "human potential" argument, let's do a little exercise (it's one I sometimes use at corporate speaking events, so it works great with groups, like if you're reading this book with a book club—hint, hint).

Think about the people you work with. If your job is inside the home or you don't have coworkers, think about a group of people with whom you regularly interact, perhaps the people you volunteer with or other parents you interact with to make things happen at your kids' school. Now, mentally break these folks into the following three categories: high performers, middle performers, and low performers.

For anybody who says, "This doesn't apply to me because everyone I know and work with is super awesome," let me offer a quick thought. No matter how high performing your team may be, virtually every group can be differentiated into these three groups. The Chicago Bulls won the NBA Championship in 1991, 1992, 1993, 1996, 1997, and 1998, all with the same basic team nucleus. Now, who was the highest performer on that team? Even non-basketball fans know the answer is Michael Jordan. Who was the next highest performer? Scottie Pippen.

Even just taking into account those two all-time great players, there was a significant difference in their respective performance. There were certainly middle performers on those teams, but I won't bother to name them. (All right, the truth is I don't really remember all their names. And if I only name two or three I'll miss the rest, but that's just further evidence that they were, in fact, middle performers.) And there were also low performers, most of whom rode the bench or got traded. So, if one of the best professional basketball teams in history has high, middle, and low performers, it's a safe bet that your teams and work associates do too.

Now that you've identified the high, middle, and low performers in the group, here's the exercise. Jot down some of the characteristics of the low performers. That is, if somebody asked you to describe why you consider this person to be a low performer, what would you say? For example, you might say he or she is negative, or stirs up trouble, or only does the bare minimum, and so forth. If you're having trouble deciding who's a low performer, here's a quick exercise: ask yourself who causes you the most emotional pain. While there can be different types of low performers, more often than not these people function like emotional vampires. They don't usually suck your blood, but they will suck the life out of you. (Although I hear vampires are cool again, so who knows what they'll do?) These are the folks that make you glad when there's rush hour traffic because it gives you a few extra minutes by yourself in your car without having to deal with them.

Now turn to the high performers and jot down some of the characteristics that distinguish them from everyone else. If you're having trouble identifying your high performers, just think about the people you turn to when things get tough, the ones who come through, no matter what. If you could choose work colleagues like you used to choose kids for kickball, no question about it, you'd choose these folks first.

So what does your list look like? When I do this as a quick group exercise, I typically get lists that describe low performers using descriptors like these: negative, me-first, they drag their feet, do the bare minimum, gossip, stir up trouble, dramatic, bring problems instead of solutions, never volunteer, more concerned with getting credit than getting things right, make excuses and blame others, bristle at getting feedback, just to name a few. The high-performer lists include descriptors like these: they always give 100 percent, they don't just identify problems—they solve them, they teach others how to be better, stay calm under pressure, positive attitude, embrace change, always looking for ways to improve, and so forth.

What stands out from these lists is that overwhelmingly the characteristics that define both high and low performers are attitudinal, not intellectual. When you really stop to think about what separates high and low performance, it's rare to say, "Low performers are just lacking in ability." Just as it's similarly infrequent to have somebody say, "High performers are just smarter." In fact, I guarantee you that at least some of the best people you work with have lower IQs than some of the worst people you work with. Believe it or not, there are some international chess masters with below-average IQs.

The people who make your team successful are not usually any smarter than anyone else. And the coworkers that make your life really difficult aren't somehow lacking in IQ points (royal pains, yes; morons, no). In the real world, raw talent isn't the predominate determinant of success. What matters way more is desire, hardiness, work ethic, and a striving to tackle big (and difficult) challenges.

K. Anders Ericsson is a professor at Florida State University and one of the top researchers on expertise. He's the first person to debunk the idea that it's somehow natural talent that determines what people can achieve. He says, "The traditional assumption is that people come into a professional domain, have similar experiences, and the only thing that's different is their innate abilities. There's little evidence to support this. With the exception of some sports, no characteristic of the brain or body constrains an individual from reaching an expert level."[1]

*Fortune* editor Geoff Colvin wonderfully distills and expands the work of Ericsson and other leading expertise researchers in his book *Talent Is Overrated*.[2] And he uses this as evidence to prove the point that a "lack of talent" is quite simply not a valid excuse for not doing big things.

In most of life, attitude does matter more than aptitude. Why? Because if you have the right attitude, you can tackle your HARD Goals while significantly increasing your aptitude. Consider a 1992 study Colvin refers to that sorted 257 music students by instrument, age, gender, and income. Researchers asked study participants about their musical precociousness, how much they practiced, and which of the nine standard levels of musical performance they had achieved at school. Here's big finding number one: no profound or conclusive measurement of early musical ability was found to correlate with top musical performance. Big finding number two was that the top students practiced for two hours a day, versus the 15 minutes a day that the lowest-performing students were giving over to practice.

Colvin notes that, by age 18, top violin students have accumulated thousands of hours of practice. The best have more than 7,000 practice hours, average players have around 5,000, and third-level musicians have only about 3,400 hours. Listen, I know how appealing it is to just say, "But those other people are just naturally talented. That's why they can do those really difficult things." Sorry, but the facts just don't back up that line of thinking. In an overwhelming majority of cases, the highest achievers are more motivated, harder working, and focused on tackling more difficult challenges.

Neither Tiger Woods nor Wolfgang Amadeus Mozart arrived into this world magically gifted. In fact, both had fathers that were ferociously driven pedagogues who invested innumerable hours training their sons, instilling within them similarly ferocious work ethics. No matter where you look, attitude begets aptitude. And, as demonstrated by those really smart but low-performing pains-in-the-posterior with whom we sometimes work, virtually no amount of aptitude can offset a really lousy attitude.

So what's the point of all this? Difficult goals are well within your reach as long as you've got the right attitude to carry them through. You already have whatever innate talent is necessary. You may not yet have learned all the skills you need, but we'll tackle that issue in just a few paragraphs. And after you've gotten through this book, you'll have the tools you need to find the drive, motivation, passion, or whatever you want to call it to pursue that HARD Goal with all your heart.

# HOW DIFFICULT IS DIFFICULT?

About 40 years ago, two psychologists dramatically advanced the science of difficult goals. We owe a lot to the brilliance of Edwin Locke and Gary Latham (and the legions of researchers they inspired). Their scientific studies involving more than 40,000 subjects provided conclusive validation that people who set or are given difficult specific goals achieve much greater performance levels than do people who set or are given weaker goals that send a message of "just do your best."

Locke and Latham's studies are too numerous to detail in this book, but there is a mix of laboratory and real-world experiments to pick from. In one of Locke's lab experiments, people were asked to correctly answer a series of math problems over two hours. (I know, the experiment itself could be construed as a difficult goal.) Some were told to "just do your best," to "get as many problems right as you can." Others were given a more difficult goal: namely, they were given specific scores that they should try and beat. (The numbers they were given were roughly 6 percent higher than the number of correct answers the "do your best" crowd had achieved.)

If you've been paying attention up to now, you shouldn't be surprised to learn that the difficult goals group beat the "do your best" crowd; not by a little, but by 20 percent on average. If you ease up and tell people "just try," they won't give much effort or perform very well. But challenge them with something more difficult, a goal that gets them a bit "amped up," and they'll go to town. Interestingly, the difficult goals group didn't start off all excited and competitive and then peter out during the two-hour experiment. Instead they started strong and stayed strong. In fact, while they beat the "do your best" crowd throughout the experiment, they really started clobbering them about 90 minutes into the session.

In one of Latham's experiments, drawn from his early work with Weyerhaeuser (the giant forestry, wood, and paper company), the research team studied how difficult goals could improve the performance of logging truck drivers.[3] For logging trucks, as with many commercial trucks, you really want them to be as close as possible to their maximum legal weight (otherwise you need multiple runs, which costs time, fuel, and trucks). But it's not easy to make happen; giant logs are all different sizes, they have to be fit on the trucks, weights need to be accurate, and so on.

For this experiment, it was determined that a load that was 94 percent of the maximum legal net weight would be difficult, but not impossible to achieve. When workers were given a "do your best" goal, they loaded the trucks to somewhere around 60 percent of the maximum legal weight (lots of wasted space). But when they were given the significantly more difficult goal of loading the trucks to 94 percent of their maximum legal weight, lo and behold, that's exactly what happened. I should note that usually experiments like this cost money (scientists aren't free). But this one simple experiment, conducted in Oklahoma, actually saved the company around $250,000.

It doesn't much matter what the situation is; setting difficult goals leads to better performance. Even in a study of brain-damaged patients at a rehabilitation hospital, difficult goals led to better performance.[4] The patients were given series of arithmetic problems, and after three series they were assigned to a difficult goals group or a "do your best" group. The difficult goals group was told, "on the last three blocks, you correctly solved X problems per block. Now we want you to improve your performance by 20 percent." And the "do your best" group was told . . . well, you know. Amazingly, on the very next round of arithmetic problems, 31 percent of the group that was given the 20 percent more difficult goal actually hit that goal. But fewer than 9 percent of the "do your best" crowd improved their performance by 20 percent.

I don't want to overdo the examples, but I do want to reiterate the point that having difficult goals will increase your performance. Whether you're growing a business, losing weight, training for the Olympics, quitting smoking, advancing your career, loading logging trucks, doing math, or rehabbing following a brain injury, the more difficult the goal, the better your performance will be.

---

## WHY DO DIFFICULT GOALS WORK?

Difficult goals work because they force us to pay attention; we can't simply sleepwalk through them. Now maybe they arouse our attention because they're a little scary, or really exciting, or they're just a big departure from our normal daily routine. But whatever the reason, they get our brains worked up. And molecular biologist John Medina tells us explicitly that "the more the brain pays attention to a given stimulus, the more elaborately the information will be encoded—and retained."[5]

It also helps to remember that your brain is getting bombarded with requests for attention all day long. Maybe even as you're reading this book an e-mail comes in, a friend texts you, your boss walks into your office, or your kids call you for dinner. (By the way, if your boss walks into your office, you're allowed to put down the book—I like career preservation as much as the next guy. But for everything else, feel free to keep reading.)

All of these events, not to mention all the background thoughts just floating around inside your head, are competing for your brain's precious attentional resources. It's like running too many applications on your computer; they consume limited resources and everything starts to slow down. But when you set a difficult goal, it consumes so much of your brain's resources that it crowds out a lot of other less important stuff. It's like shutting down some of those background computer applications. And with that extra brainpower comes better performance.

But it's not just the brain's resources that are affected; feelings get involved as well. Leadership IQ conducted a study to see how being assigned a difficult goal at work made people feel. We asked more than 4,000 people a series of survey questions such as the following:

I will have to exert extra effort to achieve my assigned goals for this year.
I will have to learn new skills to achieve my assigned goals for this year.

The first thing we discovered was that when people gave high scores on those questions, they also tended to give high scores on some of the other survey questions like the following:

I consider myself a high performer.
The work I do makes a difference in people's lives.

From this survey we were able to deduce that when people are given goals that require extra learning and effort (difficult goals), they are more likely to consider themselves high performers and also to believe that the work they do is important.

What's the explanation for this? Here are two: first, difficult goals instill confidence. I mean nobody is going to give difficult goals to a dummy. You'd only give difficult goals to somebody who had a real shot at hitting them. So, by extension, if your boss gives you a difficult goal, he or she must believe you can achieve that goal. It's another way of the boss saying, "I believe in you, I trust you, you're the right person for this job."

And, of course, this same lesson applies to parenting every bit as much as managing. You've probably seen plenty of examples where parents with multiple kids are tough on one kid while they let the other slide by not doing much (sometimes this coincides with an oldest/youngest split). Of course, the kid who gets pushed harder is ticked off at the time, but ultimately he or she grows up to be a much higher achiever and with a deeper sense of having been respected by the parents. The coddled kid gets the easier path for a few years, but he or she achieves less in later life, is less independent, and often wonders, "Why didn't they think I could do those things too?"

The second reason difficult goals work so well is that they convey the message that your work is important. Nobody would spend the time or energy to create difficult goals for work that was dumb or wasteful. For instance, you're not likely to hear, "You know that report we produce that nobody ever reads? The one that only gets produced because 100 years ago the founder used to like to verify the calculations from his abacus; you know the report I mean? Well, let's convene a team with a goal of making this dumb report take 10 minutes to complete instead of its current 20 minutes. It will test the very limits of kindergarten math and data entry typing, but let's go for it!" Puh-lease. Note: Plenty of companies set lots of dumb goals, but they typically don't receive the level of scientific attention and effort that we're talking about in this book. Dumb goals are usually of the thoughtless variety.

There was one other noteworthy finding from this study: employees who had bosses that set more difficult goals were way more likely to give high scores to the following questions:

> I recommend this company to others as a great place
>     for people to work.
> I recommend my boss to others as a great person to
>     work for.

This makes pretty good intuitive sense. If your boss really thinks through what kinds of goals are going to elicit your best performance, if he or she sits down with you to design optimally difficult goals, it's a clear indication that the boss must care about you. And that level of caring can buy a lot of heartfelt employee loyalty, not to mention a great deal of extra effort.

Think about the greatest teacher you ever had. It's a safe bet that this person cared about you and even pushed you to be your very best. I know, we all enjoyed those days when we walked into class and saw a substitute teacher and the movie projector, but the do-nothing routine would've gotten old pretty fast. And we would've been a lot worse off over the rest of our lives without the learning and pushing we got from that caring teacher.

I remember one woman I spoke to who had had a pretty rough start to life. Despite a rather abusive and chaotic home life, she made it through high school (though only on a song and a prayer). Not surprisingly, she then made it her business to run into every wrong person she could possibly find in life and got into all kinds of trouble—went looking for it, really. Then one day, via a series of circumstances, she found herself in a community college classroom and the teacher was telling her she had potential, putting books in her hands, encouraging her to pick herself up and do something that merited her intelligence. And so she became something, she now finds value in her life. And you know what she told me? "Every so often I send that teacher a postcard. I tell him, 'Look at me, I'm doing this that or the other great thing, and truly, I have you to thank for so much of it.'" It's a touching story, especially if you're an educator, but it's not unique. And great teachers don't always appear in a classroom setting. They're everywhere; you just have to keep an eye out for them. And sometimes we're our own best teachers.

## LEARNING VERSUS PERFORMANCE GOALS

I do have to mention one caveat to setting difficult goals, and it occurs if you have absolutely no idea what you're doing. For example, let's imagine that you've never played piano. (Obviously, if you really have never played piano, no imagination is necessary.) Now, let's say I give you a goal of playing an intermediate piece, like Beethoven's "Für Elise." (If you don't know

the piece, look it up online, and I'm sure you'll immediately recognize the tune.) Given such a challenge, you'll probably stare
at the music for a time, try to figure out the notes, and bit by
bit start to cobble together a few phrases. But your technique
will stink, you won't get the right fingerings, it'll be sloppy, and
even if you make your way through a few lines, you'll be greatly
undercutting your long-term ability to play piano. If I give you a
goal to play "Für Elise" and you don't know how to play piano,
a normal human will take every shortcut available to play that
piece, even if it means using lousy techniques and developing
some terrible habits.

If you don't golf and I give you a goal of breaking 100, you'll
buy every wonder club, try every swing gimmick, get the biggest
driver, buy all the magazines, and so forth. And not only will
you probably not break 100, but you won't even learn the fundamentals, like a slow backswing, keeping your head down, proper
extension, and so on. The first golf teacher I had when I was a kid
made it very clear to me: no fancy drivers until you've mastered a
5 iron. And yet, every 100-plus golfer on the planet has the coolest,
biggest driver available, with which they hit good drives maybe 10
percent of the time (all the while defiling the fundamental mechanics of a golf swing and destroying their hopes for future success).

Now, in those piano and golf examples, the inevitable failures are not the result of setting difficult goals; they're the result
of setting performance goals. Performance goals are those that
focus on getting some desired end result, like a golf score under
100 or playing "Für Elise." By contrast, a learning goal would
mean that you're less concerned with breaking 100, and more
concerned with learning the necessary fundamentals (so that
you'll eventually break 100).

When you're truly starting at ground zero, when you have
absolutely no idea how to do what you're trying to do, a perfor-

mance goal can backfire. If you can read music and you know the difference between a driver and a 3 wood, you're probably ready for performance goals. But if you think a key opens doors and a driver is the guy picking you up at the airport, well then you probably want to start with a learning goal.

Earlier in this chapter I said that most of the time, when we have trouble achieving goals, it's more about motivation than it is about ability. And that's still the case. But every so often you might encounter a situation for which you really have no skills, where you don't know a single thing you need to know in order to achieve that goal. If you have some idea what you're doing, even if you still need to learn more, you're probably ready for performance goals. If your performance goal is well designed, you're still going to do a lot of learning. Learning goals are better for situations where you're starting at the beginning—like if I asked you to solve a differential equation, and all you heard was Charlie Brown's teacher saying, "Wha-wha-wha-wha-wha."

In those cases where you're truly starting at the beginning, your best bet is to make your goals difficult, but in a learning way. If you don't know how to golf or play piano, don't say, "I'll go break 100 or bang out a little Chopin." Those are performance goals, and they probably won't work if you truly have no strategies for accomplishing those goals. So instead say, "I'm going to master the backswing and keeping my head down and keeping my body centered, and I'm going to practice each aspect 100 times, while analyzing and correcting each practice." That's a difficult learning goal, and once you've accomplished it you'll be in a much better position to move on to tackling those big performance goals.

Keep in mind that learning goals can be every bit as difficult as performance goals. Remember the study I cited earlier that found the best violin students have more than 7,000 practice hours by age 18, average players have around 5,000, and third-level musicians have only about 3,400 hours? Well, when they were first learning violin, many of those practice hours were spent on learning goals, not performance goals. And the best kids set significantly more difficult learning goals for themselves; hence the greater numbers of practice hours and the significantly better performance.

## TESTING YOUR GOALS

So now, to get very practical, how difficult should we make our goals? To answer this question, we need to do two things: first, we need to assess how difficult we typically make our goals, and second, we need to adjust our typical goals up or down to find the sweet spot of difficulty.

Let's begin by figuring out whether you have a pattern of making your goals too easy, or in those more rare cases, you make your goals too hard. To put it another way, you need to know if you're an undersetter or an oversetter. Start by thinking about the goals you've set, or attempted to set, in the past year or two; the more similar they are to your current goals, the better.

Now think about the initial goals you set, and then take a look at what you ended up achieving. For example, let's say I've set three running goals in the past few years. In case 1, I set a goal of running a three-mile race but ended up running a six-mile race. In case 2, I set a goal of running a six-mile race, but because things were moving along better than I had originally thought, I ended up running a nine-mile race. And in case 3, I set a goal of running a six-mile race and I ended up running that six-mile race, but it wasn't super hard and I got a personal best time. If this is my history, it's safe to say that I pretty consistently underset my goals.

I could do this with my company, where every year I say we're going to grow by 20 percent, and yet our actual yearly growth is more like 30 percent. I could also do this with weight-loss goals, savings goals, and so on. A lot of people underset goals, and whether intentional or not, it's like we're "padding" our goals. We can slack off a bit and still hit the original target because we set that original target under what we are actually capable of achieving (hence the label *undersetter*). Much of the time you can even estimate a rough percentage by which you underset your goals. In the company example, if I say we'll grow by 20 percent but we grow by 30 percent, and this happens pretty regularly, I'd be consistently undersetting my goals such that I'd need to increase my goals by 50 percent if I want them to reflect the reality of my actual achievements.

It works exactly the same with oversetting goals too. If I consistently say I'll run 10 miles and I get to 5 miles, or I say I'll save 12 percent a year but I really save 6 percent, or whatever, then I'd be oversetting my goals such that I'd need to reduce them by 50 percent if I want them to more closely approximate reality.

The point is this: make your goals with as much precision as you can, because you can't scientifically tweak them if you don't begin with an accurate picture. If I'm a track coach and I'm supposed to turn you into a world-class runner, I need to know how fast you really run so I can design the proper workouts. If you tell me, "I can run a five-minute mile," and I build your workouts around that figure, you won't make any real progress if it turns out that you can actually run a four-minute mile.

This kind of sandbagging happens all the time, and business processes are prime examples (budgets, order fulfillment, time lines, and the like). Do you know the phrase "underpromise and overdeliver"? Well, that's exactly what I'm talking about; it sounds good, but it's really just undersetting our goals. And it just destroys our ability to use a more scientific goal-setting process to get the kinds of results we're all dying to see.

In the next step, we're going to take this newly accurate goal and subject it to two simple questions: what am I going to learn from this goal, and how do I feel about this goal? For the first question, ask yourself, "How is this goal going to stretch me?" More specifically, what will you have to learn to achieve your goal? How will you grow as a person as a result of your goal? What new skills will you have acquired by virtue of pursuing your goal? If you remember our earlier discussion about performance versus learning goals, I said that even when a goal is a performance goal, you should still be learning all sorts of wonderful things. And that's exactly what we're testing here.

An appropriately difficult goal, one that puts you right in that sweet spot of difficulty, is going to require you to learn. It's going to stretch your brain, excite some neurons, amp you up, and awaken your senses. If you can breeze through a goal without learning, it's just not difficult enough. So how much learning is enough learning? Well, go back to the very beginning of the chapter when I asked you to describe your greatest personal accomplishments and use that as your measuring stick. You need to be learning about that much for this goal. Another way to think about this is that a goal has the right level of difficulty when you're going to have two to four major new learning experiences from it.

What if your goal isn't going to generate that level of learning and growth? That's a sign that you need to make your goal about 30 percent more difficult. Given that we took the sandbagging out of our goals, making a goal 30 percent more difficult is usually enough to get our brain excited and start those neurons firing. And of course, if you still need more difficulty, take it up another 30 percent. Just don't start arbitrarily tripling or quadrupling the difficulty of your goal, because that can very quickly take it from optimally difficult to just plain impossible.

Kevin Andrews is the president of SmartBen, a software company that developed a cutting-edge platform for benefit administration and employee self-service. Every human resources executive in the world knows of the company, but in layman's terms, it delivers a Web-based platform whereby the employees of a company can view and manage their salary, benefits, retirement planning, and more. Now, that's all well and good, but it's not what makes Kevin and his company interesting. What makes them worth talking about is what happened when they got too successful.

SmartBen's client roster reads like the Fortune 500, and the company is brilliantly run (in other words, it's very profitable). But after several years of being in business, the company's leaders didn't have the same electric buzz that they did when their company was a start-up. To hear Kevin tell it, "I felt like we were stagnating. Yes, we were financially successful and our clients were happy, but we felt a bit flat. I'd come into work without much enthusiasm and leave the same way. My brain just wasn't getting switched on at work."

So one day Kevin was on a plane and picked up a scientific magazine a previous passenger had left in the seat pocket. It was a fortuitous happening as the magazine was all about artificial intelligence (you know, computers developing consciousness and talking to you, and so on). Kevin's technical brain immediately woke up, and he was riveted. By the time the plane landed he was tweaked like a coffee addict and he knew exactly what he was going to do: "The answer was so obvious," Kevin said. "I had stopped learning. We had gotten so successful that I just wasn't learning enough." And so, fueled by the idea that using a science that was truly on the cutting edge (artificial intelligence) would sufficiently activate his own brain, he set out to create the smartest software the human resources world had ever seen.

There are self-service technologies that allow corporate employees to manage their health benefits or whatever. But there aren't any besides SmartBen that have a digital person appear on the screen and talk to you. "Ben AI," as he's known, uses artificial intelligence programming to analyze all of an employee's benefits, retirement savings, salary history, and more and makes smart recommendations. He literally looks at you and tells you how you could more effectively save for retirement and what it would do to your paycheck. And if employees want to collaborate with him, they can use the interface to model their own changes; for example, to pick the right health plan for their family's unique requirements. The net effect is that the employees make much smarter decisions, pick plans that are totally right for them—which makes them much happier, and the company saves money with all the efficiency.

But all of this awe-inspiring technology belies how incredibly difficult it really was to achieve. "We had to rethink every aspect of how we design, develop, and code," says Kevin. "We had to move from traditional programming to real cutting-edge, almost sci-fi, approaches. We were literally thinking years beyond everyone else in the industry." There were days his brain hurt; days he questioned the "smartness" of this approach. "But I'll say this," he says, "my brain was alive. I hadn't felt this pumped about something since we started the company. We didn't know what we were doing at first, but we learned every day. And now we've got people coming to us because we've become so expert."

Although I don't think his computers have developed their own independent consciousness, there were moments when I test-drove their system when I wasn't sure. In fact, Kevin told me, "It sounds crazy, but as we continue to develop the algorithms, we keep having these 'aha' brainstorms. It's almost like the program wants us to keep learning, to keep getting smarter."

You don't necessarily need to go create artificial intelligence algorithms to keep your brain active. (For me, I'd end up with way too many *Terminator* and *Matrix* dreams). But you do have to push yourself to learn something, to keep your brain alive and lit up.

The second test involves another pretty simple question: To what extent is this goal within my comfort zone? Let me give you some choices for your answer:

1. Totally within my comfort zone ("Don't worry, I could do this with my eyes closed.")
2. Pretty much within my comfort zone ("I'm awake, but hardly in a state of excitement.")
3. A little outside of my comfort zone ("I feel a little twinge of excitement or nervousness.")
4. Outside my comfort zone ("I'm on pins and needles, totally bug-eyed alert.")

5. So far outside my comfort zone I'm too dumbfounded to even respond ("I'm in such a terror-stricken state I can't even think.")

This test is pretty subjective and requires a personal judgment call, but the most effective goals are going to be somewhere around choice 4. Choices 1 and 2 are way too easy, and choice 5 is way too hard. But choice 3 is getting close, and choice 4 is right on the money.

If you think back to our exercise at the beginning of the chapter, you probably said that your greatest achievements were outside of your comfort zone. You also most likely said that when you were just starting to pursue that great achievement you had some doubts about whether or not you'd be able to pull it off. It's pretty much definitional: if your goal is sufficiently easy that you have no doubts about your ability to achieve it, then it can't be that important a goal. But if your goal is so grand that its achievement warrants a mention among the top few great accomplishments in your life, then it's going to make you feel a twinge of excitement, nervousness, or something.

If you answered the above question with choice 1 or 2, it's a sign that you need to make your goal another 20 percent more difficult. If you answered with choice 5, make it 20 percent less difficult. More often than not, if you fixed your goal properly with the first test (how will this goal stretch you?), then you'll need less tweaking here. And thus, you'll typically need to make smaller adjustments to your goal (in other words, adjusting by 20 percent instead of 30 percent).

The whole point of this exercise is to get you into that sweet spot of difficulty. Because when you make your goal too easy, while you may hit your target, it won't be significant enough to make a real difference in your life (or your company or your family or whatever). Or you'll get bored with it and not even bother seeing it through to fruition. And if you make your goal too difficult, then it's likely to end up on the scrap heap of abandoned goals, like a free trial to the gym a few months after New Year's.

---

## WHAT HOLDS US BACK FROM DIFFICULT GOALS?

Notwithstanding everything we've covered so far, there's still one big issue that could hold you back and prevent you from set-ting (and attempting) your difficult goals: they're intimidating. If you have a fear of anything—spiders, snakes, heights, open spaces, commitment, or germs, to name a few—you know how scary it can be to even think about trying to overcome that fear, usually because you have to experience the fear to overcome it. Even difficult goals that aren't nearly as intimidating as these other fears can still make the average person hesitate, and even back off.

Listen, if advancing your career, starting a business, dou-bling sales revenue, losing weight, running a marathon, quit-ting smoking, going back to school, and saving more money were easy goals, everybody would be doing them. But everybody doesn't do these things, and that's why the fact that you're even reading this book puts you in a pretty select group of people who share both the drive and the vision for greatness.

What makes difficult goals so intimidating? The short answer is a fear of failure. In theory, the more difficult your goal becomes, the higher the possibility that you could fail. Now, every study I cited earlier in the chapter says that won't happen. The more difficult your goal, the better your performance is likely to be. In fact, it's because the difficult goal gives you a jolt, stimulates your brain, gets you out of your comfort zone, and excites you emotionally that you're able to deliver your best performance. But all that notwithstanding, a sizeable group of folks are still fundamentally afraid that if they attempt a difficult goal they might fail. (And given many people's history with poorly designed goals that were doomed to fail from the get-go, perhaps that's a pretty understandable thought process.)

So how do we overcome that fear of failure? How do we mentally get ourselves over that hump of trepidation (or anxiety or fear or whatever you want to call it)? With a pretty simple process that's going to rewire the way we think. We tapped into the emotional parts of our brain in the "Heartfelt" chapter and the visual parts in the "Animated" chapter. In this chapter, we're going to be using the logical/analytical parts of our brain.

Step 1 of this process requires asking yourself a very simple question: "What happens to me if I fail at this goal?" I say it's a simple question, but that doesn't mean it's an easy question. Answering it truthfully requires a deep look into some of your inner mental processes.

When I'm working with someone (or an entire organization) to figure out what they're really afraid will happen if they fail at this goal, here are the kinds of answers I hear:

- People will think I'm weak and couldn't hack it.
- I'll be exposed as someone who talks a good game but can't deliver.
- People will be disappointed in me.

- People will never believe in me again.
- I'll never believe in myself again.
- I'll die from embarrassment.
- If I can't do this, it means I'll never be able to do anything.
- It'll mean that I'm not as smart/talented/skilled as I like to think I am.
- This is my only shot at this. (In other words, it's now or never, you only get one bite at the apple, and so forth.)
- It means I'm stuck in this state forever.

There are two big problems with these statements. First, often when we describe what will happen to us if we fail, we use words like *never, always, only, die.* These are serious and highly charged words, and they reflect a deep level of fear. Saying, "I'll die of embarrassment if I fail to achieve this goal" is probably a bit of an overstatement when we assess the actual facts. But it is a true reflection of how intensely we feel these fears (even if we don't acknowledge that intensity at a conscious level).

It's not unexpected for us to feel a fear of failure, but the intensity of our feelings can often rival or even exceed the fear we feel from things that might truly kill us. When a fear of failure stops us from tackling a goal, 99 percent of the time the fear we feel is very different from the fear we'd feel if a saber-toothed tiger were charging at us.

Some fear is very healthy. From an evolutionary perspective, being afraid of saber-toothed tigers, lions, and spiders kept us alive. But there are times in this modern world, far away from the dangers of actual saber-toothed tigers, that our fear reactions get pointed to something quite abstract, and perhaps even imagined. If you fail in your goal to escape a saber-toothed tiger, you will almost certainly be dead minutes later. But if you fail in your goal to increase your savings this month, you've got at least a decent chance of still being alive 30 minutes later. Most of the repercussions we face if we fail in achieving our goals are not going to kill us.

Not only will we not actually die of embarrassment, we might not even have cause for any embarrassment (let alone enough to kill us). It's important to note that the statements on our list of "what happens to us if we fail" are not proven facts; they're interpretations, assumptions, emotionally charged extrapolations, castastrophizing, irrational beliefs, or whatever else you want to call them. But they are not proven facts.

Let's prove this with Step 2 of our process. We're human beings, not computers, so we can't just flip a switch and say, "Oh, feeling like I'll die of embarrassment is irrational, so I'll just stop feeling that way." Instead, we've got to debunk these thoughts in our heads, just as if we were attorneys from "Law & Order" cross-examining a witness. So we're going to take each of these statements and, one by one, ask ourselves if we can find any examples that might provide evidence to the contrary of what we said.

Let's take the example, "If I fail to achieve my goal, I'll die from embarrassment." Can you find any examples in your life (or even someone else's life) where you failed to achieve a goal but didn't die? To take it a step further, can you find any examples where any embarrassment you felt was far less than what you were expecting? Now, by virtue of your being alive and reading this book right now, I'm guessing you found at least one example that refutes the belief that "I'll die from embarrassment."

Of course, that was a pretty easy example to counter, so let's try something more difficult. How about, "If I fail at this goal,

people will think I'm weak and couldn't hack it." Again, search
your history, or someone else's history, for counterarguments.
I've got plenty of examples personally, but let's take somebody
with more dramatic goals: Lance Armstrong. Lance is a guy
with difficult goals—he's a 38-year-old guy with kids trying to
make a comeback in cycling. As I write this book, one of his
specific difficult goals is to win the Tour of California (like the
Tour de France, but less famous). But he crashed and is out of
the race, so let's call that a failed difficult goal. But does anybody really think Lance is weak? Have we abandoned him? Do
we think he'll never be able to do anything again? Do you think
he believes that?

I would argue that Lance is a pretty good counterargument
to the idea that failing at a difficult goal means people will think
you're weak. Heck, if anything, the guy's probably got more
supporters because he's showed his humanity and his struggles,
and who doesn't love to root for that?

We literally need to take those "what happens to us if we
fail" statements and debunk them, one by one. Use your analytical brain and your life history. I'm confident that if you take
every one of them apart you'll find they hold no real power.

Once you've finished that exercise, the final step is to rewrite
those statements. You've debunked them, so now turn them
around into something a lot more encouraging. For example,
here are some revised statements:

- If I fail at this goal, people won't think I'm weak. In
  fact, they may even rally to my defense.
- If I fail at this goal, people will still believe in me.
- If I can't do this specific goal, it has no bearing on my
  ability to tackle other difficult goals.

You've disproved the negative statements you started with, so it's just a question of closing the loop and cementing this logically sound bit of encouragement in your consciousness. Overwhelmingly, we have little or nothing to fear from attempting (and even failing at) a difficult goal, because it's only by attempting difficult goals that we hone our ability to successfully achieve them. And remember, we'll have absolutely no control over our lives and destinies if we're paralyzed by the fear of the mostly imagined consequences of failing at difficult goals.

---

## SUMMARY

Just doing your best doesn't cut it in the world of HARD Goals. But how difficult is difficult enough? Well, if your current HARD Goal doesn't measure up to all those things you've felt in the past when doing something great, increase the difficulty. Shake that brain up, make it register the message that you're a high performer, that you can make a difference, that your goal is required. Because the more difficult your goal, the more necessary it's going to feel and the better performance you're going to deliver.

And if your goal demands you start from scratch and learn a whole host of new skills, well, just create a HARD learning goal to get yourself up and running. Then, before you know it, you'll be swapping over to HARD performance goals. And if you have a history of making your goals too easy (an undersetter) or too hard (an oversetter) pay attention to that fact and make adjustments early on. Ask yourself, "What am I going to learn from this goal and how do I feel about this goal?" If you're not learning, if you don't feel totally amped up, you're not in your HARD Goal sweet spot.

You should feel outside your comfort zone, not so far that you feel like you're on a bed of nails, but not too comfortable either. You'll know when you find your sweet spot, because you've been there before, and it's that place where you achieve your absolute best. And those fears that pop up now and then, don't dodge them. Look them square in the eye and evaluate how much validity they really have. Are you really going to die of embarrassment if you don't achieve your goal? Nothing rips the power away from fear quite like a good debunking.

Get more examples and tools at hardgoals.com.

# Conclusion: Starting Your HARD Goal

As I've said throughout the book, implementing a goal gets a lot easier when that goal is HARD. Executing a goal you don't care about—that doesn't stimulate your heart or mind—really requires a superhuman effort. And given the shocking failure rates for most goals (like the more than 80 percent who abandon their New Year's resolutions), a goal that isn't HARD will probably fail. And all the computerized reminders and notes tacked on the fridge won't save it.

However, when a goal activates your brain, touches your heart, pushes you to grow, and is an existential necessity, you are absolutely going to implement that goal. In fact, you'll smash through every roadblock on earth to do so. Not only will computer reminders and sticky notes be unnecessary, they'll seem comically trivial.

When first starting to implement your HARD Goals, it might take a little push to get the techniques covered in this book into action. As a result of some serious experimentation over the years, I've discovered a technique that works well to kick-start the implementation of any HARD Goal. This technique, which I call Cutting in Half, is especially useful if this is the first time you're consciously setting a HARD Goal.

---

## CUTTING IN HALF

The first step is to take an objective long view of your HARD Goal and approximate its end date. Some goals are more naturally time-bound than others, but as accurately as you can, estimate the time frame by which you'll have completed your goal. To keep things simple for this example, I'm going to pretend that your HARD Goal will take you a year to accomplish (but again, Cutting in Half works with goals of any duration).

Now, cut that time frame in half (six months in this example) and answer this question: What must I have accomplished at the six-month mark in order to know that I'm on track to achieve the full HARD Goal? Let's imagine my goal is to run a marathon, that's 26.2 miles, in one year (and of course, I've addressed all the requisite heartfelt, animated, required, and difficult aspects). What do I need to have accomplished at six months in order to be on track for the full marathon in one year? Let's say I need to have reached a long run of 13 miles, be charting four runs per week, and have learned how to fuel during a long run. (By the way, do you see how easy it would be to abandon this goal if all I had was a bunch of mileage numbers and I didn't have all the underlying heartfelt, animated, required, and difficult aspects already in place?)

Now, cut that six-month time frame in half (three months) and answer this question: What must I have accomplished at the three-month mark in order to know that I'm on track to achieve all of my six-month targets? Maybe you need to have long runs of five miles, know how to use a heart rate monitor, fit into size medium running shorts, or be able to run while your kids bike alongside of you for four miles on the local trail.

Of course, you know what's coming next. Cut that three-month time frame in half and answer, what must I have accomplished at the six-week mark in order to know that I'm on track to achieve all of my three-month targets? When you've got it spelled out, do it again: What must I have accomplished at the three-week mark in order to know that I'm on track to achieve all of my six-week targets?

Now, once you've gotten to a time frame under one month, do this exercise two more times. Ask yourself, what must I have accomplished within this next week in order to know that I'm on track to achieve all of my three-week targets? And then ask yourself, what must I have accomplished today in order to know that I'm on track to achieve all of my one-week targets?

The purpose of this exercise is threefold: first, it shows you exactly where and how to start pursuing your HARD Goal. Second, it monitors and keeps you on track to achieve your HARD Goal (and intensify your efforts where necessary). And third, this exercise shows you that every single day needs to contain some activity in pursuit of your HARD Goal.

This process is not a replacement for your HARD Goal. In fact, the only way you'll do the stuff for today and next month, and all the rest, is if you're being mentally fueled by a powerful HARD Goal. This process is just here to help you prioritize your first steps. HARD Goals can be, well, hard. So this breaks your HARD Goal down, not into easy steps, but into clearly identifiable steps.

## CALL A FRIEND

Once you know what your first steps need to be, and specifically what you need to do today, there's one more technique that can help keep you on track.

A few years ago I was leading a retreat for a group of eight CEOs to help them create HARD Goals. You probably know a few of them, but all are high-powered leaders who get together a few times a year to think, share, brainstorm, and push each other. And so, with the justification of needing uninterrupted thinking space, they decided to hold this retreat in Anguilla. (I'm not going to lie; sometimes travel is tough, and sometimes it's not.)

After a particularly intense day of goal setting and strategizing and challenging each other, one member of the group (I'll call him Pat) says, "I'm bought-in. I desperately need this goal, it will change my life. But I also feel like an alcoholic. What if I get back to civilization and all the seemingly urgent stuff starts to crowd out the really important stuff like this HARD Goal? What if I can't stop myself from taking that drink or attending that stupid meeting or checking my e-mails all day?"

Well, that was a showstopper. Honestly, at that point, all I wanted to do was end the session and catch an hour on the beach with a stiff drink. But then, before I could even respond, one of the other group members (let's call him Chris) said something that totally changed my thinking. Chris said, "Pat, if you feel like an alcoholic, I'll be your sponsor. I'll call you for five minutes every single day and check in on you. And since I have the same fears as you, you can check in on me too."

Remember, there were eight CEOs at this retreat. Within three seconds of Chris's comments, the other six people had paired up to do the same thing. It was so simple, so obvious, so easy, and yet it just hadn't occurred to me, or anyone else I knew. Making things even easier, all their secretaries had spoken to each other plenty of times, so they just assigned making the daily calls to them (their assistants were truly expert at making their bosses stop what they were doing for something important like this).

Now, these CEOs weren't going to respond to judgmental nagging any better than you or I do. So rather than having their friend call and badger them about not getting enough done, they added a new twist: they would all write five to seven questions about their HARD Goal that they wanted that friend to ask them when he or she called.

Four of the questions were basically prompts about the elements of their HARD Goals. For Heartfelt, they might ask, "Why do you care about your goal?" For Animated, the question might be, "Tell me how it looks or feels when you hit your goal." For Required, they might ask, "Why is this goal necessary right now?" And a Difficult question could be, "What are you learning because of this goal?" These questions are important because they all knew that the more they thought about their HARD Goals, the more integrated into their lives the goals would become. They weren't calling to chat and ask, "How's your day?" One and all wanted to nicely, but powerfully, ensure that each person's HARD Goal remained seared in his or her mind.

Then, the other one to three questions would be of the "What did you do today to advance your goal?" variety. Remember the earlier Cutting in Half exercise? Well, they basically started with the question, what must I have accomplished today in order to know that I'm on track to achieve my HARD Goal? And then they took specific issues and made those the questions for their friend to ask. For example, maybe the friend would ask, "How many miles did you run today?" or "What was your heart rate?" or "Describe the quality time you spent with your kids?" or "What did you do to develop a subordinate?" or "Describe what you ate." The questions were specific to each person's HARD Goal, and because it was their goal, each person could make up whatever questions he or she wanted.

The point of all this is very simple: keep your HARD Goals front and center in your mind and use them to crush any mental roadblocks that might emerge.

As I said at the very beginning of this book, you might have doubts about achieving big goals, but I don't have any doubts about your impending achievements. As soon as you opened this book, I knew you were after greatness, significance, and meaning. And I know you've got the talent and mind-set to achieve it. Now, having gone through this book together, you've got HARD Goals—goals that are finally worthy of your significant gifts.

That first step is yours to take. And trust me, the first step is not a doozy. It's a giant leap to the life you want and deserve.

# Notes

**CHAPTER 1**

1. Lyle Nelson, interview by author, May 2010.
2. Roland G. Fryer Jr., "Financial Incentives and Student Achievement: Evidence from Randomized Trials" Harvard University, EdLabs, and NBER, April 8, 2010).
3. Amanda Ripley, "Should Kids Be Bribed to Do Well in School?" *Time*, April 8, 2010, http://www.time.com/time/nation/article/0,8599,1978589-3,00.html.
4. Tess Koppleman, "Real Life Superman Saves Young Girl's Life," *Chicago Tribune*, December 18, 2009, http://www.chicagotribune.com/news/wjw-supermansaveslitte girl,0,570673.story.
5. Andreas Bartels and Semir Zeki, "The Neural Correlates of Maternal and Romantic Love" (Wellcome Department of Imaging Neuroscience, University College London, November 13, 2003), *NeuroImage* 21 (2004): 1155–1166.

6.  Amos Tversky, *Preference, Belief, and Similarity: Selected Writings* (The MIT Press, Cambridge, MA, 2003).

7.  Ibid., 888.

8.  Deborah A. Small, "Sympathy and Callousness: The Impact of Deliberative Thought on Donations to Identifiable and Statistical Victims" (University of Pennsylvania, March 3, 2006), http://sciencethatmatters.com/wp-content/uploads/2007/04/small06sympathy.pdf.

9.  Maurice R. Schweitzer, "Beware the Harmful Effects of Goal-Setting," *Bloomberg Businessweek*, April 3, 2009.

10. "Our Philosophy," Google Corporate Information, http://www.google.com/corporate/tenthings.html.

11. Susan J. Curry and Edward H. Wagner, "Evaluation of Intrinsic and Extrinsic Motivation Interventions with a Self-Help Smoking Cessation Program," *Journal of Consulting and Clinical Psychology* 59, no. 2 (1991): 318–324.

12. Kevin G. Volpp et al., "A Randomized, Controlled Trial of Financial Incentives for Smoking Cessation," *The New England Journal of Medicine* 360, no. 7 (2009): 699–709.

13. E. Tory Higgins et al., "Increasing or Decreasing Interest in Activities: The Role of Regulatory Fit," *Journal of Personality and Social Psychology* 98, no. 4 (2010): 559–572.

14. M. R. Lepper, D. Greene, and R. E. Nisbett, "Undermining Children's Intrinsic Interest with Extrinsic Reward: A Test of the 'Overjustification' Hypothesis," *Journal of Personality and Social Psychology* 28 (1973): 129–137.

15. "The engineer's life," Google Jobs, http://www.google.com/jobs/lifeatgoogle/englife.html (accessed July 26, 2010).

16. "28 Days of Holiday Gift Ideas—Day 9," *Hollywood Today*, December 5, 2009, http://www.hollywoodtoday

.net/2009/12/05/28-days-of-holiday-gift-ideas
-%E2%80%93-day-9 (accessed July 26, 2010).

## CHAPTER 2

1. John Medina, *Brain Rules: 12 Principles for Surviving and Thriving at Work, Home, and School* (Seattle: Pear Press, 2008), 234.

2. Chris Delp and Jeffrey Jones, "Communicating Information to Patients: The Use of Cartoon Illustrations to Improve Comprehension of Instructions," *Academic Emergency Medicine* 3, no. 3 (2008): 264–270.

3. Deborah Nelson and Kim-Phong L. Vu, "Effects of a Mnemonic Technique on Subsequent Recall of Assigned and Self-Generated Passwords," *HCI* 8 (2009): 693–701.

4. Nanci Bell, *Visualizing and Verbalizing: For Language Comprehension and Thinking* (Nancibell Inc, 2007).

5. Sarah Blaskovich, "Success Stories—Brian Scudamore: Trash Is His Treasure," *Success* magazine, http://www.successmagazine.com/success-stories-brian-scudamore/PARAMS/article/688.

6. Stephen J. Hoch, Howard C. Kunreuther, and Robert Gunther. *Wharton on Making Decisions* (New York: Wiley, 2004).

7. Carmine Gallo. *The Presentation Secrets of Steve Jobs: How to Be Insanely Great in Front of Any Audience* (New York: McGraw-Hill, 2009).

8. John Medina, *Brain Rules* (Seattle: Pear Press, 2008).

9.  Allan Paivio, "Mental Imagery in Associative Learning and Memory," *Psychological Review* 3 (1969): 241–263.

10. John Jacob O'Neil, *Prodigal Genius: The Life of Nikola Tesla* (Albuquerque: Brotherhood of Life, 1994), 257.

11. Richard P. Feynman, *Surely You're Joking, Mr. Feynman! (Adventures of a Curious Character)* (New York: W.W. Norton & Company, 1997).

## CHAPTER 3

1.  T. J. Potts, "Predicting Procrastination on Academic Tasks with Self-Report Personality Measures" (doctoral dissertation, Hofstra University). *Dissertation Abstracts International* 48 (1987): 1543.

2.  J. Harriott and Joseph R. Ferrari, "Prevalence of Procrastination among Samples of Adults," *Psychological Reports* 78 (1996): 611–616.

3.  Joseph R. Ferrari, Kelly L. Barnes, and Piers Steel, "Life Regrets by Avoidant and Arousal Procrastinators: Why Put Off Today What You Will Regret Tomorrow?" *Journal of Individual Differences* 30, no. 3 (2009): 163–168.

4.  R. Neal Axon, W. David Bradford, and Brent M. Egan, "The Role of Individual Time Preferences in Health Behaviors Among Hypertensive Adults: A Pilot Study," *Journal of American Society of Hypertension* 3, no. 1 (2009): 35–41.

5.  Suzanne B. Shu and Ayelet Gneezy, "Procrastination of Enjoyable Experiences," *Journal of Marketing Research*,

2010. http://www.marketingpower.com/AboutAMA/
Documents/JMR_Forthcoming/Procrastination_Enjoyable
_Experiences.pdf.

6. Richard H. Thaler and Shlomo Benartzi, "Save More
Tomorrow: Using Behavioral Economics to Increase
Employee Saving," University of Chicago and The Anderson School at UCLA, July 2003. http://economics.uchicago
.edu/download/save-more.pdf.

7. Sheena S. Iyengar and Mark R. Lepper, "When Choice
Is Demotivating: Can One Desire Too Much of a Good
Thing?" *Journal of Personality and Social Psychology* 79,
no. 6 (2000): 995–1006.

8. Sheena Iyengar, G. Huberman, and W. Jiang, "How Much
Choice Is Too Much? Contributions to 401(k) Retirement
Plans," in *Pension Design and Structure: New Lessons
from Behavioral Finance*, ed. O. S. Mitchell and S. Utkus
(Oxford University Press, 2004), 83–95.

9. Dan Ariely and Klaus Wertenbroch, "Procrastination,
Deadlines, and Performance: Self-Control by Precommit-
ment," *Psychological Science* 13, no. 3 (2002): 219–224.

10. Irwin P. Levin et al., "A Tale of Two Pizzas: Building Up
from a Basic Product Versus Scaling Down from a Fully-
Loaded Product," *Marketing Letters* 13, no. 4 (2002):
335–344.

## CHAPTER 4

1.  Christopher Percy Collier, "The Expert on Experts," *Fast Company*, November 1, 2006.

2.  Geoff Colvin, *Talent Is Overrated: What Really Separates World-Class Performers from Everybody Else* (New York: Portfolio Hardcover, October 2008).

3.  Gary P. Latham and J. James Baldes, "The 'Practical Significance' of Locke's Theory of Goal Setting," *Journal of Applied Psychology* 60, no. 1 (1975): 122–124.

4.  Siegfried Gauggel and Jutta Billino, "The Effects of Goal Setting on the Arithmetic Performance of Brain-Damaged Patients," *Archives of Clinical Neuropsychology* 17 (2002): 283–294.

5.  John Medina, *Brain Rules* (Seattle: Pear Press, 2008). 74.

# Index

ments, Murphy was a three-time nominee for *Modern Health-care*'s Most Powerful People in Healthcare Award, joining a list of 300 luminaries including George W. Bush and Hillary Clinton. Only 15 consultants had ever been nominated to this list. He was also awarded the Healthcare Financial Management Association's Helen Yerger Award for Best Research.

A seasoned public speaker, Murphy has illuminated audiences for hundreds of groups and lectured at the Harvard Business School, Yale University, the University of Rochester, and the University of Florida.

For free downloadable resources about this book, including quizzes and discussion guides, please visit hardgoals.com.

# About the Author

M ark Murphy is the founder and CEO of Leadership IQ (www.leadershipiq.com). Since its inception, Leadership IQ has become a top-rated provider of goal-setting training, leadership training, employee surveys, and e-learning. As the force behind some of the largest leadership studies ever conducted, Leadership IQ's programs have yielded remarkable results for such organizations as Microsoft, IBM, MasterCard, Merck, MD Anderson Cancer Center, FirstEnergy, Volkswagen, and Johns Hopkins. Murphy's cutting-edge leadership techniques and research have been featured in *Fortune*, *Forbes*, *Businessweek*, *U.S. News & World Report*, the *Washington Post*, and hundreds more periodicals. He was featured on a CBS News "Sunday Morning" special report on slackers in the workplace as well as being featured on ABC's "20/20." He has also made several appearances on Fox Business News.

Murphy's previous book was the international bestseller *Hundred Percenters: Challenge Your People to Give It Their All and They'll Give You Even More*.

A former turnaround advisor, Murphy guided more than 100 organizations from precarious financial situations to record-setting levels of prosperity. For these and other accomplish-